ONDORI
EASY CROSS-STITCH

CONTENTS

★ Copyright © 1984 ONDORISHA PUBLISHERS. LTD., All rights reserved.
★ Published by ONDORISHA PUBLISHERS, LTD.,
   32 Nishigoken-cho, Shinjuku-ku, Tokyo 162, Japan.
★ Sole Overseas Distributor : Japan Publications Trading Co., Ltd.,
   P. O. Box 5030 Tokyo International, Tokyo, Japan.
★ Distributed in the United States by Kodansha International/ USA Ltd.
   through Harper & Row, Publishers, Inc., 10 East 53rd Street, New York, New York 10022.
   Australia by Bookwise ; 1 Jeanes Street, Beverley, South Australia 5009, Australia.

10 9 8 7 6 5 4 3 2 1

ISBN 0-87040-604-3
Printed in Japan

BREEZE AND I

Instructions on page 60.

2   Instructions on page 58

Instructions on page 52

3

For Your Private Time

Left : Instructions on page 65.
Top : Instructions on page 64.
Bottom : Instructions on page 68.

Left : Instructions on page 69.
Top : Instructions on page 106.
Bottom : Instructions on page 74.

Left : Instructions on page 72.
Center : Instructions on page 75.
Right : Instructions on page 82.

Actual Size Photo

Left : Instructions on page 83.
Right : Instructions on page 80.

Actual Size Photo

Top : Instructions on page 116.
Bottom : Instructions on page 77.

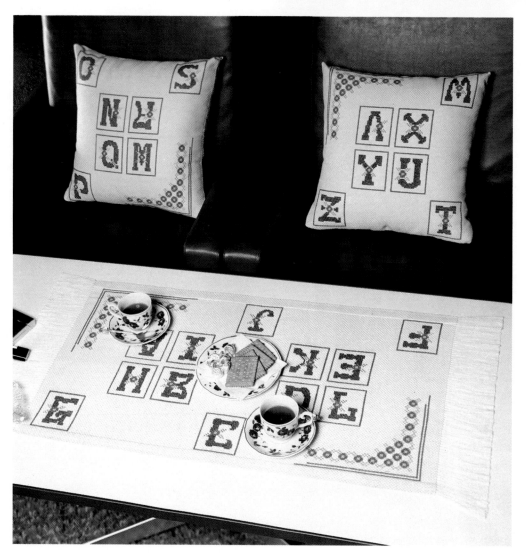

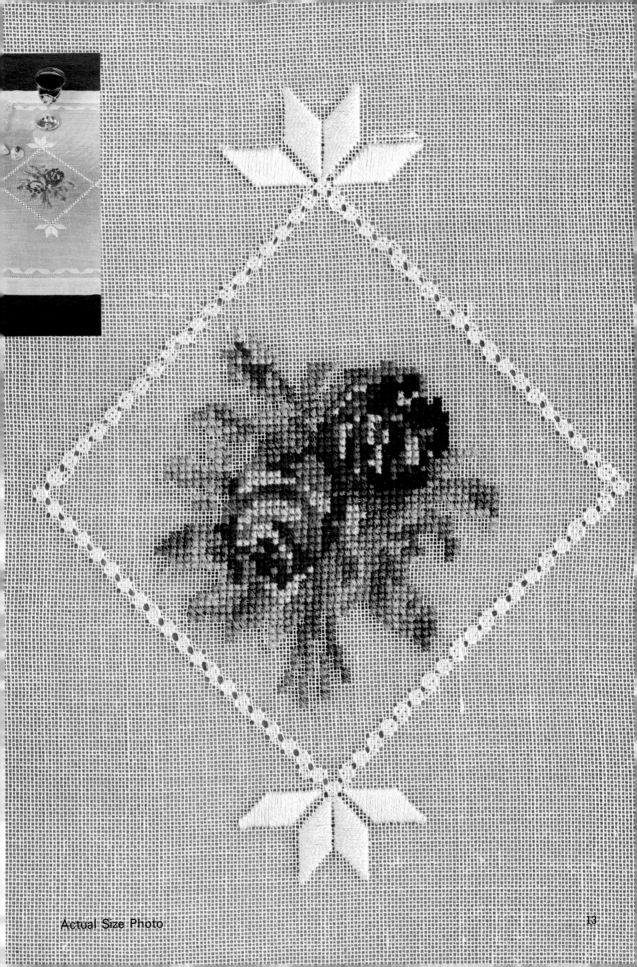

Actual Size Photo

When You Relax With Tea

Left : Instructions on page 88.
Top : Instructions on page 89.
Bottom : Instructions on page 89.

Top : Instructions on page 86.
Bottom : Instructions on page 87.

Close-up Photo

Close-up Photo

MAKING YOUR ROOM SPECIAL

Left : Instructions on page 104.
Top : Instructions on page 94.
Bottom : Instructions on page 96.

Top : Instructions on page 95.
Bottom : Instructions on page 96.

They Come From a Fairy Land

Instructions on page 91.

Top : Instructions on page 107.／Bottom : Instructions on page 100.

Top : Instructions on page 103. ╱ Bottom : Instructions on page 102.

Tips of Idea For Gifts

Instructions on page 26.

PILLOWS, shown on page 25

Materials: Each of Black and Red Aida cloth (35 vertical and horizontal threads per 10 cm square) 85 cm by 44 cm/Inner Pillow 88 cm by 45 cm, stuffed with 450 gr kapok (for each)/40 cm-long zipper.
THREADS: DMC 6-strands embroidery floss:
For Red Pillow
3 skeins of Kelly Green (701); 2 skeins each of Parakeet Green (906), Plum (552), Electric Blue (996, 995), Canary Yellow (972), Black (310); 1 skein each of Geranium Red (754), Hazel-nut Brown (869).
For Black Pillow
3 skeins of Kelly Green (701); 2 skeins each of Parakeet Green (906), Flame Red (608), Brilliant Red (666), Electric Blue (995), Canary Yellow (972), Geranium Red (754), Hazel-nut Brown (869).

Finished size: 41 cm square.
Directions: Use 6 strands of floss throughout. 1-thread square is counted for each stitch in the chart. Find embroidery area in the fabric, and work cross-stitches, following the chart. Sew in the zipper as indicated. Fold the embroidered piece with the right sides facing, and machine-stitch. Put in the inner pillow, after stuffing it with kapok.

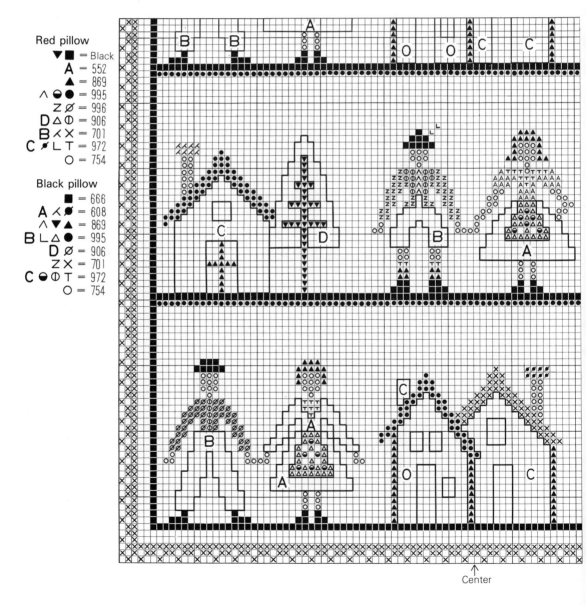

Red pillow
▼■ = Black
A = 552
▲ = 869
∧ ◒ ● = 995
Z Ø = 996
D △ ⦶ = 906
B ✗ ✕ = 701
C ✐ L T = 972
O = 754

Black pillow
■ = 666
A ✗ ✎ = 608
∧ ▼ ▲ = 869
B L △ ● = 995
D Ø = 906
Z ✕ = 701
C ◉ ⦶ T = 972
O = 754

Center

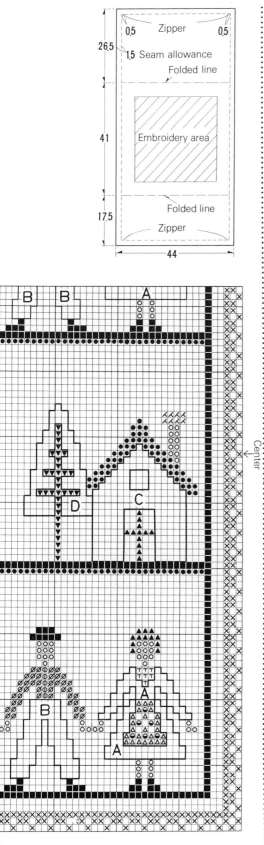

Materials: Beige Indian cloth (51 vertical and horizontal threads per 10 cm square) 16 cm by 15 cm/Picture frame 11 cm by 10 cm (inside).

THREADS: DMC 6-strand embroidery floss: 1/2 skein each of Avocado (472, 471, 469), Pistachio Green (368, 367, 320), Almond Green (504, 503, 502), Indian Red (3042), Dull Mauve (778); small amount each of Coffee Brown (801), Umber (739, 435, 434, 433), Smoke Gray (822, 644, 642), Beaver Gray (648, 646), Moss Green (937), Cardinal Red (347), Rust Red (918), Indigo (336), White and Black (310).

Fisnished size: Same as the frame.

Directions: Use 4 strands of floss throughout. 1-thread square is counted for each stitch in the chart. Find the center point of both the chart and fabric, and begin from that point. Put the picture in the frame.

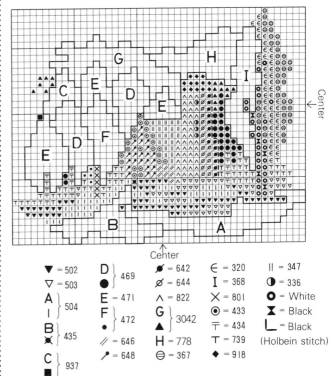

▼ = 502	D } 469	⌀ = 642	€ = 320	‖ = 347
▽ = 503	● } 469	∅ = 644	I = 368	◑ = 336
A } 504	E = 471	∧ = 822	✕ = 801	O = White
I } 504	F } 472	⊙ = 433	✕ = Black
B } 435	• } 472	⊤ = 434	L = Black
✖ } 435	∥ = 646	H = 778	T = 739	(Holbein stitch)
C } 937	⚲ = 648	⊖ = 367	◆ = 918	
■ } 937				

27

Left : Instructions on page 30.
Right : Instructions on page 112.

PILLOWS, shown on page 28

Materials: (for each) Beige Java cloth (25 vertical and horizontal threads per 10 cm square) 83 cm by 55 cm / Inner Pillow 80 cm by 53 cm, stuffed with 430 gr kapok / 49 cm-long zipper.

THREADS:

For Left Pillow

DMC 6-strand embroidery floss: 4-1/2 skeins of Magenta Rose (962); 3 skeins of Beaver Gray (645); 2-1/2 skeins of Green (3051); 1-1/2 skeins each of Scarab Green (3347), Episcopal Purple (718); 1 skein each of Fire Red (900), Saffron (725), Umber (738), Black (310); small amount each of Beige Brown (840), Gernet Red (309). Anchor 6-strand embroidery floss: 1 skein of Cornflower Blue (119).

For Right Pillow

DMC 6-strand embroidery floss: 4 skeins of Greenish Gray (597); 3 skeins of Beaver Gray (645); 2-1/2 skeins of Green (3051); 1-1/2 skeins each of Black (310), Forget-me-not Blue (824), Magenta Rose (962), Scarab Green (3347); 1 skein each of Umber (738), Forget-me-not Blue (825); small amount each of Garnet Red (309), Golden Yellow (783).

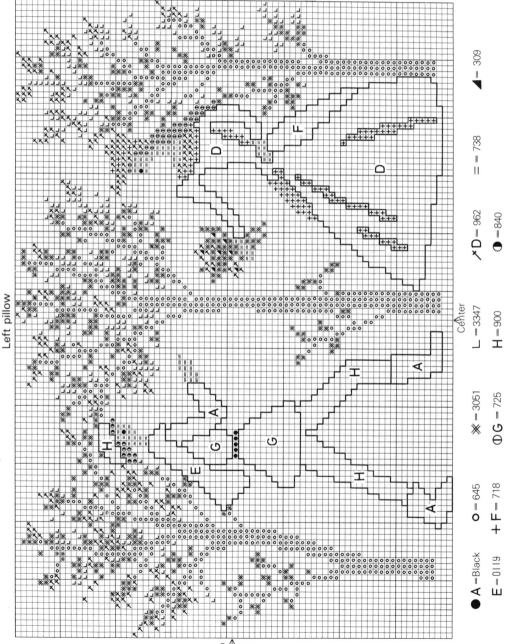

Left pillow

Center

Center

▲ = 309
= = 738
✗ D = 962
◑ = 840
L = 3347
H = 900
✳ = 3051
◐ G = 725
O = 645
+ F = 718
● A = Black
E = 0119

Directions: Use 9 strands of floss throughout. 1-thread square is counted for each stitch in the chart. Work following the chart. Sew in the zipper, and put the stuffed inner pillow in the embroidered pillow.

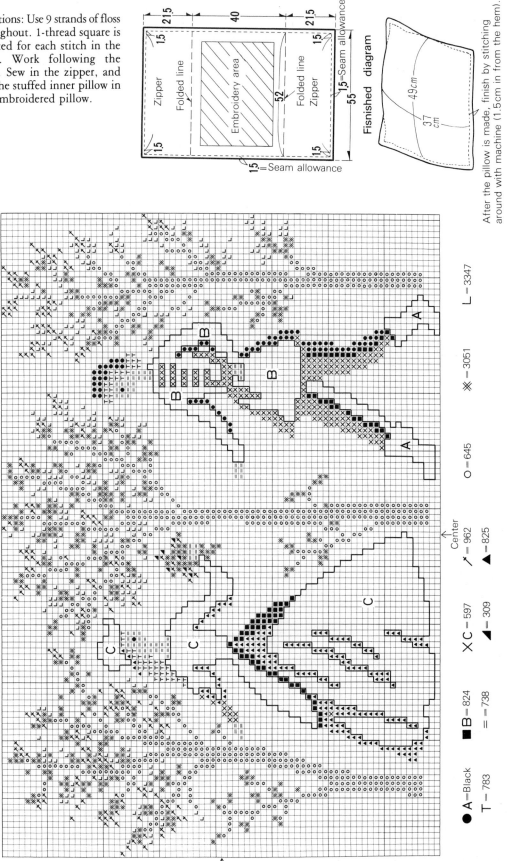

Fisnished diagram

After the pillow is made, finish by stitching around with machine (1.5cm in from the hem).

Right pillow

Center

Center

● A=Black   ■ B=824   X C=597   ◢ =309   ↗ =962   O=645   ※ =3051   L =3347

T =783   = =738   ▲ =825

Top of the Left : Instructions on page 34.
Bottom of the Left : Instructions on page 34.
Top of the Right : Instructions on page 27.
Bottom of the Right : Instructions on page 43.

Oval

Materials: Canvas cloth (80 vertical and horinzontal threads per 10 cm square) 9.5 cm by 7 cm/Picture Frame 8.5 cm by 6.2 cm in Oval (inside).
THREADS: DMC 6-strand embroidery floss: 1 skein of Myrtle Gray (928); 1/2 skein each of Garnet Red (335), Soft Pink (3326), Scarlet (815), Lilac (208), Army Green (3052, 3051), Khaki Green (3012, 3011); small amount of Dark Yellow Gold (725). Anchor 6-strand embroidery floss: 1/2 skein each of Old Rose (42), Cerise(59), Violet Mauve (107), Parma Violet (105); small amount each of Dark Lilac (112), Cornflower Blue (119).
Finished size: Same as the frame.
Directions: Use 3 strands of floss throughout. 1-thread square is counted for each stitch in the chart. Fill the outer space in blue gray.

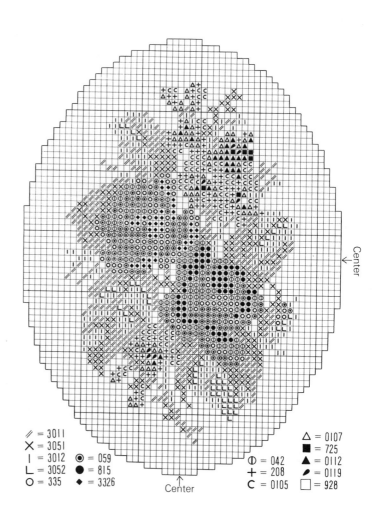

Center

Center

∥ = 3011		△ = 0107	
✕ = 3051		■ = 725	
I = 3012	◉ = 059	▲ = 0112	
L = 3052	● = 815	✎ = 0119	
○ = 335	◆ = 3326	□ = 928	
	◐ = 042		
	+ = 208		
	C = 0105		

Bottom, Left

Materials: Canvas cloth (80 vertical and horizontal threads per 10 cm square) 9 cm square/Picture frame 7 cm diameter (inside).
THREADS: DMC 6-strand embroidery floss: 1-1/2 skeins of Ecru; 1/2 skein each of Forget-me-not Blue (826, 824), Violet Mauve (327), Dark Lilac (552), Garnet Red (326), Fuschia Pink (601), Peacock Green (991), Emerald Green (912); small amount each of Dark Yellow Orange (742), Black (310).
Fisnished size: Same as the frame.
Directions: Use double strands of floss throughout. 1-thread square is counted for each stitch in the chart. Find the center point of each of chart and fabric, and begin working from there. After cross-stitches are completed, put the picture in the frame.

Bottom, Right

Materials: Canvas cloth (80 vertical and horizontal threads per 10 cm square) 9 cm square/Picture frame 7 cm diameter (inside).
THREADS: DMC 6-strand embroidery floss: 1-1/2 skeins of Beige (3024); 1/2 skein each of Scarab Green (3346), Parakeet Green (905), Avocado (471), Light Yellow (3078), Kelly Green (704), Yellow Green (734); small amount each of Canary Yellow (971), Golden Yellow (783), Black (310).
Finished size: Same as the frame.
Directions: Use double strands of floss thoughout. 1-thread square is counted for each stitch in the chart. Find the center point of the embroidery area, and begin cross-stitches from that point.

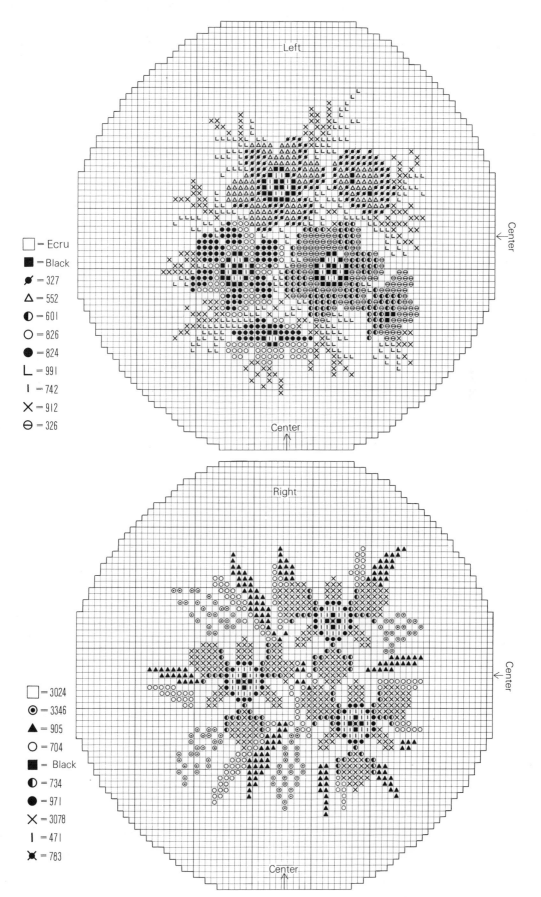

Left

Center

□ = Ecru
■ = Black
✎ = 327
△ = 552
◑ = 601
○ = 826
● = 824
L = 991
I = 742
✕ = 912
⊖ = 326

Center

Right

Center

□ = 3024
◉ = 3346
▲ = 905
○ = 704
■ = Black
◑ = 734
● = 971
✕ = 3078
I = 471
✖ = 783

Center

35

Top : Instructions on page 114./Bottom : Instructions on page 38.

Top : Instructions on page 109./Bottom : Instructions on page 109.

ALBUM, shown on page 36

Bottom

Materials: Beige Indian cloth (52 vertical and horizontal threads per 10 cm square) 90 cm by 40.5 cm.
THREADS: DMC 6-strand embroidery floss: 1-1/2 skeins each of Drab (611), Khaki Green (3013), Army Green (3052); 1 skein each of Old Gold (676), Ivy Green (500), Almond Green (504, 502), Moss Green (936), Peacock Green (991), Army Green (3051), Watermelon Pink (894), Garnet Red (335), Soft Pink (3326, 899), Garnet Red (326); 1/2 skein each of Dark Brown (3031), Soft Pink (818), Garnet Red (309), Scarlet (902, 815).
Finished size: 40 cm by 34.5 cm.
Directions: Use 3 strands of floss throughout. 1-thread square is counted for each stitch in the chart. Work cross-stitches, following the chart. You may need professional help fo finished album.

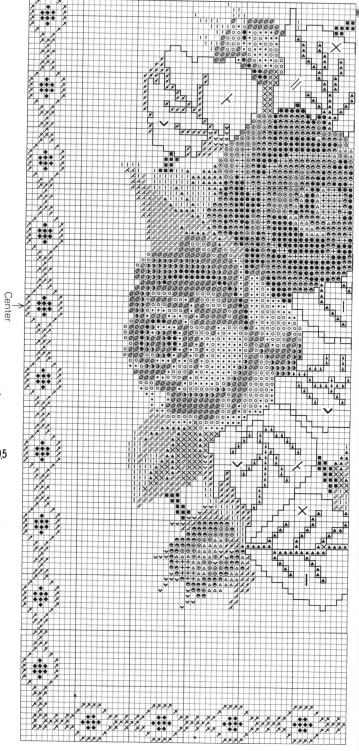

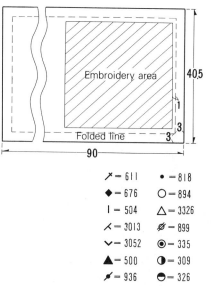

Embroidery area

Folded line

40.5

90

✗ = 611	• = 818
◆ = 676	○ = 894
I = 504	△ = 3326
✗ = 3013	∅ = 899
∨ = 3052	◉ = 335
▲ = 500	◑ = 309
✗ = 936	⊖ = 326
∥ = 991	● = 815
✗ = 502	+ = 902
↓ = 3051	
■ = 3031	

See page 114, instructions for Top.

Center

40   Instructions on page 42.

Instructions on page 42.

SLIPPERS, shown on page 40

Materials: (for 2 pairs) Single eaven-weave cloth (70 vertical and horizontal threads per 10cm square) Each of Black and Red 78cm by 30cm.
THREADS: DMC 6-strand embroidery floss:
Red Slipper
1-1/2 skeins of Cinnamon Orange (975), 1/2 skein each of White, Scarab Green (3346), Parakeet Green (907), Tangerine Yellow (740), Dark Yellow Orange (742), Medium Yellow Orange (743).
Black Slipper
1-1/2 skeins of Cinnamon Orange (975), 1/2 skein each of White, Scarab Green (3346), Parakeet Green (907), Garnet Red (309), Soft Pink (899, 776).
Finished size: Regular size.
Directions: Use 8 strands of floss throughout. 2-thread square is counted for each stitch in the chart. You may need professional help for finished slippers.

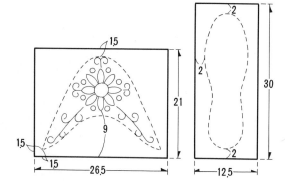

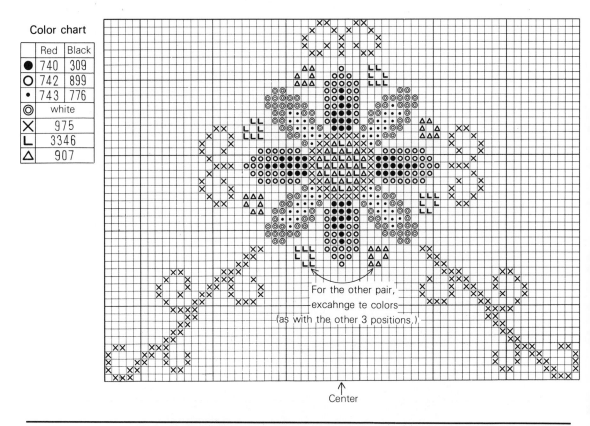

Color chart

	Red	Black
●	740	309
O	742	899
•	743	776
◎	white	
X	975	
L	3346	
△	907	

For the other pair, excahnge te colors (as with the other 3 positions.)

Center

SLIPPERS, shown on page 41

Materials: (for 1 pair) Black Aida cloth (35 vertical and horizontal threads per 10cm square) 78cm by 30cm.
THREADS: DMC 6-strand embroidery floss:
Right Slipper
1 skein each of Royal Blue (995), Plum (553), Emerald Green (912), Saffron (725); 1/2 skein each of Sky Blue (519), Moss Green (470).

Left Slipper
1 skein each of Greranium Pink (891), Cerise (601), Emerald Green (912), Saffron (725); 1/2 skein each of Soft Pink (818), Moss Green (470).
Finished size: Regular size.

Color chart

	Right	Left
◎	553	601
O	519	818
■	995	891
L		725
•		470
X		912

Directions: Use 6 strands of floss throughout. 1-thread square is counted for each stitch in the chart. Cut out the shape of slipper, and work on cross-stitches. You may ask for professional help for finishing.

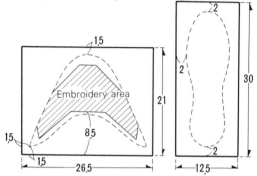

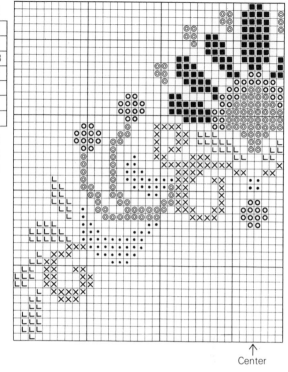

Center

MINI PANEL, shown on page 33

Materials: Beige Indian cloth (51 vertical and horizontal threads per 10 cm square) 16 cm by 15 cm / Panel frame 11 cm by 10 cm (inside).
THREADS: DMC 6-strand embroidery floss: 1/2 skein each of Moss Green (935), Avocado (472, 471, 470, 469), Copper Green (834); small amount each of Scarab Green (895), Pistachio Green (367, 320), Myrtle Gray (928), Coffee Brown (801), Umber (435, 434), Rust Red (918), Scarlet (815), Smoke Gray (644, 642), Copper Green (831), Beaver Gray (648, 646, 645), Almond Green (504), White and Black (310).
Finished size: Same as the frame.

Directions: Use 4 strands of floss throughout. Find the center point of embroidery area, and work cross-stitches. Mount and frame.

A = 935
B = 469
◉ = 470
C ⎫ 471
O ⎭
• = 472
F ⎫ 834
△ ⎭
X = 435
▼ = 895
⊕ = 367
⊘ = 320
E = 928
⬙ = 645
∅ = 646
◇ = 648

⊖ = 504
■ = 918
● = 831
λ = 801
T = 434
G = 815
∥ = 642
V = 644
D ⎫ White
ɤ ⎭
L = Holbein stitch

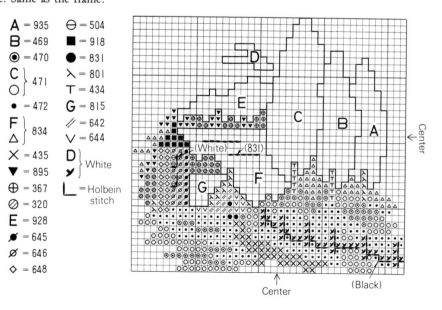

Center

(Black)

43

CHILDREN'S HANDBAGS

Left : Instructions on page 46.
Right : Instructions on page 110.

GIRL'S BAGS, shown on page 44

Top

Materials: Green Indian cloth (52 vertical and horizontal threads per 10 cm square) 70 cm by 36 cm/Cotton fabric for lining (inner bag) 57 cm by 36 cm.

THREADS: DMC 6-strand embroidery floss: 1/2 skein each of Fuschia Pink (604, 602), Lemon Yellow (444); small amount each of Fuschia Pink (603), Garnet Red (309), Dark·Yellow Orange (742), Kelly Green (704).

Bottom

Materials: Beige Indian cloth (51 vertical and horizontal threads per 10 cm square) 70 cm by 36 cm/Cotton fabric for lining 57 cm by 36 cm.
THREADS: DMC 6-strand embroidery floss: 1/2 skein each of Lilac (208), Geranium Pink (891), Black (310); small amount each of Flame Red (606), Fuschia Pink

(604, 602, 601, 600), Geranium Pink (892), Old Rose (3350), Soft Pink (3326, 819), Dark Lilac (552), Plum (554), Tangerine Yellow (740), Orange (741), Lemon Yellow (307), Coffee Brown (801), Red Brown (919), Seagull Gray (452), Umber (433), Cardinal Red (347), Jade Green (943), Scarab Green (3356), Parakeet Green

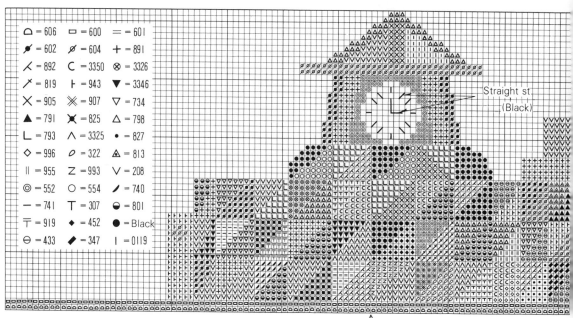

Anchor 6-strand embroidery floss: small amount each of Episcopal Purple (92, 87), Plum (98), Parma Violet (110, 105), Cornflower Blue (119), Royal Blue (133), Emerald Green (243).
Finished size: 33 cm widthwise, 24.5 cm lengthwise.

Directions: Use 3 strands of floss throughout. 1-thread square is counted for each stitch in the chart. Cut out the pieces as indicated, and work cross-stitches on the front side of the bag. Make bottom, and machine-stitch both sides. Make inner bag (lining), and join with the bag with the top hem slightly low to hide from front view. Make the straps, and sew in the bag.

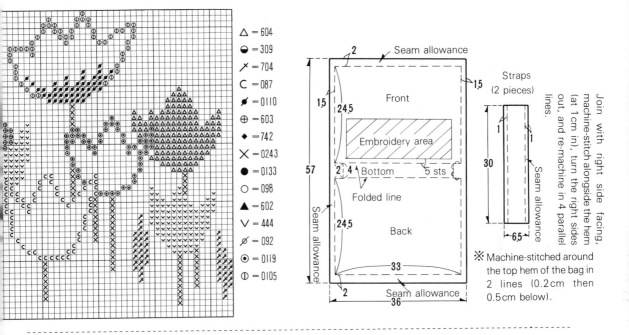

△ = 604	
◒ = 309	
✗ = 704	
C = 087	
✎ = 0110	
⊕ = 603	
◆ = 742	
✕ = 0243	
● = 0133	
○ = 098	
▲ = 602	
V = 444	
∅ = 092	
⊙ = 0119	
⏻ = 0105	

※ Machine-stitched around the top hem of the bag in 2 lines (0.2 cm then 0.5 cm below).

Join with right side facing, machine-stitch alongside the hem (at 1 cm in), turn the right sides out, and re-machine in 4 parallel lines.

(907, 905), Yellow Green (734), Emerald Green (955), Peacock Green (993), Electric Blue (996), Cornflower Blue (793, 791), Medium Blue (798), Forget-me-not Blue (827, 825, 813), Indigo (322), and Azure Blue (3325). Anchor 6-strand embroidery floss: small amount of cornflower Blue (119).

Finished size: 33 cm widthwise, 24.5 cm lengthwise.
Directions: Use 4 strands of floss throughout. 1-thread square is counted for each stitch in the chart. For making up, see the directions for the other bag.

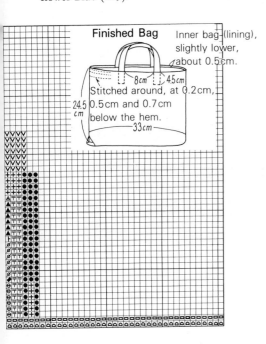

Finished Bag Inner bag (lining), slightly lower, about 0.5 cm.

8 cm 4.5 cm

Stitched around, at 0.2 cm, 0.5 cm and 0.7 cm below the hem.

24.5 cm

33 cm

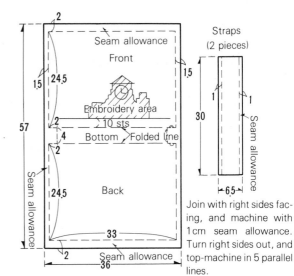

Join with right sides facing, and machine with 1 cm seam allowance. Turn right sides out, and top-machine in 5 parallel lines.

Instructions on page 50.

GIRL'S BAG, shown on page 48

Materials: White Single eaven-weave cloth (70 vertical and horizontal threads per 10cm square) 74cm by 34cm/Cotton fabric for lining 62cm by 29.5cm/Blue cotton frill 3.5cm by 110cm.
THREADS: DMC 6-strand embroidery floss: 1-1/2 skeins of Forget-me-not Blue (809); 1 skein of Saffron (725); 1/2 skein each of Geranium Red (351), Cerise (604), Brilliant Green (702), Ash Gray (414), Black (310), Mahogany (301), Indigo (311), Faded Pink (224), Moss Green (470); small amount each of Golden Yellow (782), Beige Brown (842), Soft Pink (899, 776). Anchor 6-strand embroidery floss: 1/2 skein each of Cornflower Blue (119, 117).

Finished size: 28cm widthwise, 26cm lengthwise.
Directions: Cut out pattern pieces as indicated. Use 6 strands of floss throughout. 2-threads square is counted for each stitch in the chart. Find the center point of embroidery area, and begin working cross-stitches. Insert frill piece between front and back of the bag, and machine together when you machine the around the sides. Join two straps with the bag (inserted between bag and lining). Top of the lining is slightly lower, hiding from front view.

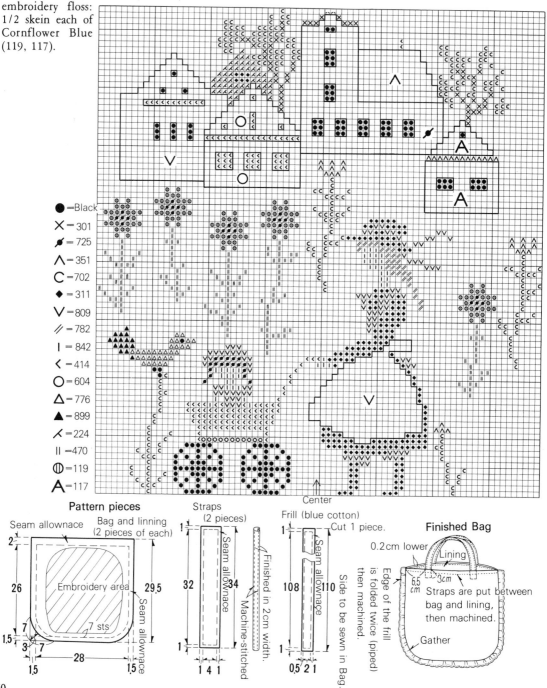

● =Black
✗ = 301
✗ = 725
∧ = 351
C = 702
◆ = 311
∨ = 809
// = 782
I = 842
< = 414
O = 604
△ = 776
▲ = 899
✗ = 224
II = 470
⦶ = 119
A = 117

Center

Pattern pieces

Bag and linning (2 pieces of each)

Seam allowance

2
26
7
1.5
3 7
1.5   1.5
28

Embroidery area

7 sts

29.5

Seam allownace

Straps (2 pieces)

32   34

Seam allownace

Machine-stitched

Finished in 2cm width.

1 4 1

Frill (blue cotton)
Cut 1 piece.

108   110

Seam allownace

Side to be sewn in Bag.

0.5 2 1

Finished Bag

0.2cm lower
Lining

6.5 cm
3cm

Edge of the frill is folded twice (piped) then machined.

Straps are put between bag and lining, then machined.

Gather

50

GIRL'S BAG, shown on page 49

Materials: Bright yellow Aida cloth (35 vertical and horizontal threads per 10 cm square) 87 cm by 35 cm/Cotton fabric for lining 71 cm by 33.5 cm.

THREADS: DMC 6-strand embroidery floss: 3 skeins of Black (310); 1-1/2 skeins each of White, Umber (738), Tangerine Yellow (741); 1 skein each of Cornflower Blue (792), Episcopal Purple (718); 1/2 skein each of Umber (433), Geranium Red (350); small amount each of Drab (612), Soft Pink (776).

Finished size: 30.5 cm widthwise, 34 cm lengthwise.
Size of stitch: 1 square of design = 1 square mesh of fabric.
Directions: Cut pattern pieces, following the directions. Use 6 strands of floss throughout. Find the center point of embroidery area, and begin working cross-stitches. Make bag, and put inner bag (lining) inside.

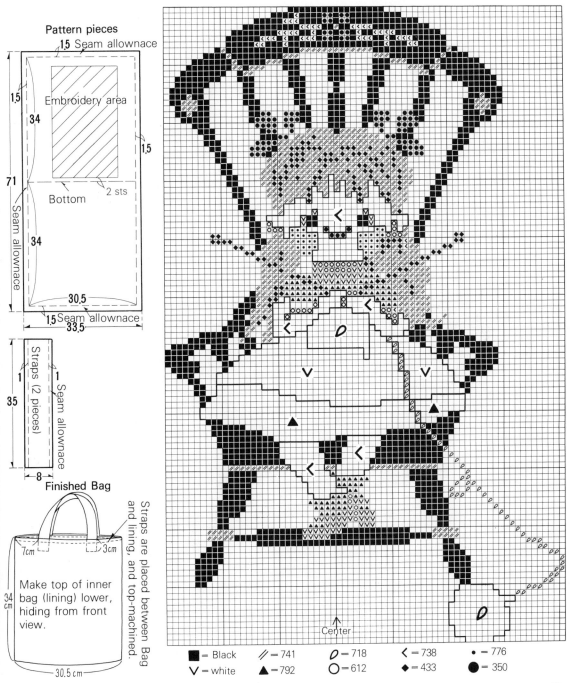

Pattern pieces

1.5 Seam allownace

Embroidery area

1.5

34

Bottom

1.5

2 sts

71

Seam allownace

34

30.5

1.5 Seam allownace

33.5

Straps (2 pieces)

35

1 1

Seam allownace

8

Finished Bag

7cm 3cm

Make top of inner bag (lining) lower, hiding from front view.

34 cm

30.5 cm

Straps are placed between Bag and lining, and top-machined.

Center

■ = Black   ∥ = 741   𝒪 = 718   ‹ = 738   • = 776
V = white   ▲ = 792   ○ = 612   ◆ = 433   ● = 350

51

INITIAL LETTERS

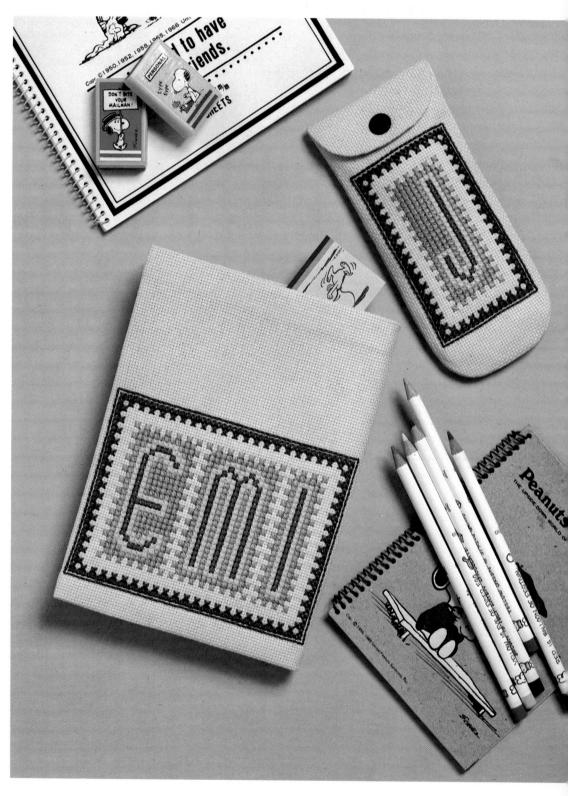

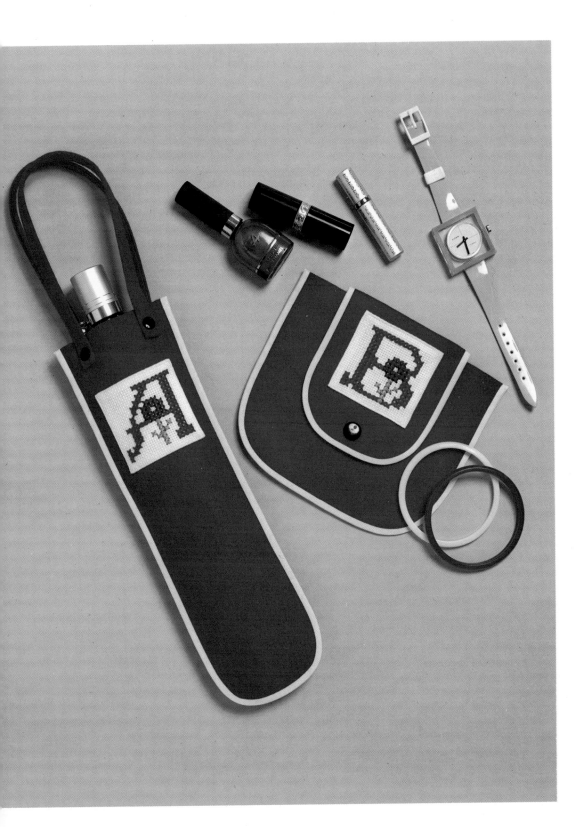

Instructions on page 55.

BOOK COVER & PEN CASE, shown on page 52

Book Cover

Materials: Beige Java cloth (60 vertical and horizontal threads per 10 cm square) 51.5 cm by 25 cm/Cotton fabric for lining 54.5 cm by 25 cm.
THREADS: DMC 6-strand embroidery floss: 1 skein each of Umber (433), Parakeet Green (907); 1/2 skein each of Lemon Yellow (307), Peacock Blue (517).
Finished size: 43.5 cm by 21 cm.

Directions: Use 6 strands of floss throughout. 2-thread square is counted for each stitch in the chart. Make a slip-proof band separately. After cross-stitches are made, join cover and lining with right sides facing, and machine. Place the slip-proof where indicated, and machine with the cover. Turn flap inside (to te size of the book), and finish with hand.

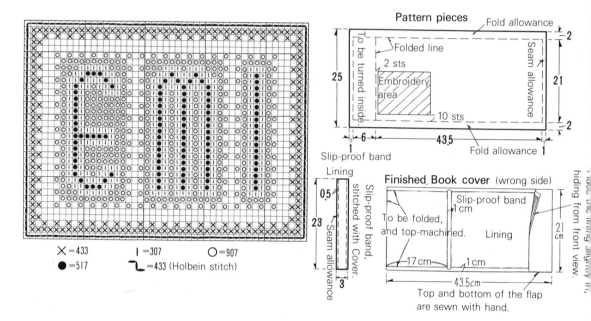

X = 433   I = 307   O = 907
● = 517   ⌐ = 433 (Holbein stitch)

Pen Case

Materials: Beige Java cloth (60 vertical and hprizontal threads per 10 cm square) 41 cm by 9 cm/Cotton fabric for lining 41 cm by 9 cm/Cardboard 8 cm by 7 cm/Dot-button for professional use, or a pair of snaps.
THREADS: DMC 6-strand embroidery floss: 1 skein of Umber (433); 1/2 skein each of Parakeet Green (907), Lemon Yellow (307); small amount of Peacock Blue (517).
Finished size: 18 cm by 8 cm.
Size of stitch: 1 square of design = 2 squares mesh of fabric.
Directions: Cut out the fabric in pattern pieces. Use 6 strands of floss throughout. After the cross-stitches are completed, make Pen Case and lining separately, to be joined later. Two equally cut cardboard pieces are placed in the flap of the case. All lining are hidden from front view. If the dot-button is not available, a pair of snaps will do.

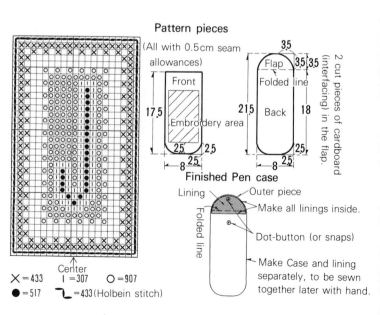

X = 433   I = 307   O = 907
● = 517   ⌐ = 433 (Holbein stitch)

PARASOL CASE & VANITY CASE, shown on page 53

Parasol Case

Materials: White Java cloth (60 vertical and horizontal threads per 10 cm square) 7.5 cm by 7 cm / Red wool fabric (lightweight) 29 cm by 34 cm / Cotton fabric for lining 19 cm by 28 cm / 1 cm-wide White bias strip 63 cm / 4 buttons (for professional use).
THREADS: DMC 6-strand embroidery floss: small amount each of Scarlet (304), Golden Green (581), Cornflower Blue (791), Lemon Yellow (444).
Finished size: 9.5 cm in width, 29 cm in depth.
Directions: 2-thread square is counted for each stitch in the chart. Use 6 strands of floss throughout. Find the center point of the embroidery area, and begin working cross-stitches from that point. Cut 2 pieces of each of Pen

Case and lining. Place the embroider piece where indicated, with edges tucked in. Join raw edges of Case and Lining (4 pieces altogether), and wrap them with bias strip. The hand straps are twice-folded then top-machined. Sew 4 ends of the straps on the case. Sew on buttons. (Ask for professional help for setting the special buttons seen in the picture.)

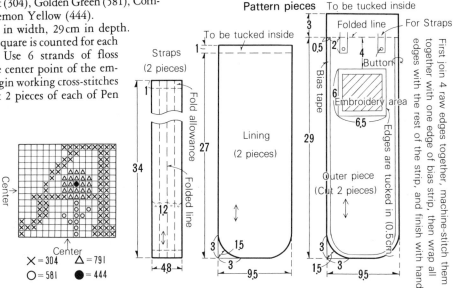

Pattern pieces

X = 304   △ = 791
O = 581   ● = 444

Vanity Case

Materials: White Java cloth (60 vertical and horizontal threads per 10 cm square) 7.5 cm by 7 cm / Red wool fabric (lightweight) 44 cm by 15.5 cm / Cotton fabric for lining 44 cm by 14.5 cm / 1 cm-wide White bias strip 70 cm / Dot-button (for professional use) 1.
THREADS: DMC 6-strand embroidery floss: small amount each of Scarlet (304), Golden Green (581), Cornflower Blue (791), Lemon Yellow (444).
Finished size: See illustration.
Directions: Use 6 strands of floss throughout. 2-thread

square is counted for each stitch in the chart. Find the center point of the embroidery area, and begin cross-stitches. Place the embroidered piece on the flap of the case, with edges tucked in. Wrap the raw edges of flap with bias strip. Join Case and lining with right sides facing, with the flap joined as indicated and machine around. Wrap the raw edges of Case and lining (with right sides out) with bias strip. You'd better ask for professional help for putting the dot-button on; otherwise a large sized pair of snaps will do.

X = 304
△ = 791
O = 581
● = 444

Pattern pieces

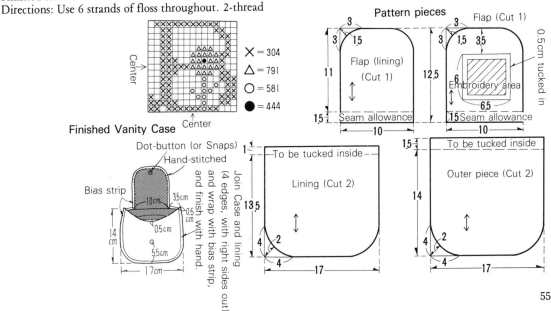

Finished Vanity Case

55

Instructions on page 57.

PLACE MAT & NAPKIN SET, shown on page 56

Materials: White Aida cloth (35 vertical and horizontal threads per 10 cm square) 42 cm by 32 cm for Place Mat and 42 cm by 40 cm for Napkin/ # 4 (1.75 mm) Crochet hook.

THREADS (For 2 pieces): Anchor 6-strand embroidery floss: 1 skein each of Peony Rose (54), Geranium Red (52), Pistachio Green (242); 1/2 skein of Episcopal Purple (87). DMC cotton thread No. 30: 20 gr of white. Finished size: Place Mat 42 cm by 32 cm/Napkin 42 cm by 40 cm.

Size of stitch: 1 square of design = 1 square mesh of fabric.

Directions: Use 6 strands of floss throughout. Work cross-stitches at one of the corners, where indicated. Fold in the hems on the wrong side of the fabric, and finish with crochet (illustration below).

Place mat

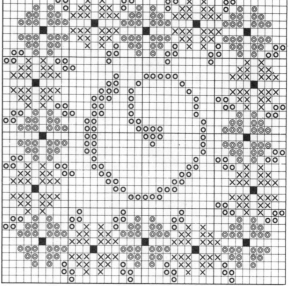

Place mat

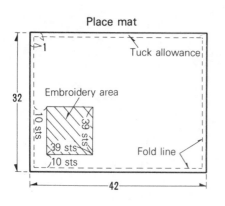

Napkin

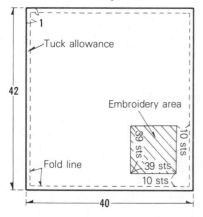

Napkin

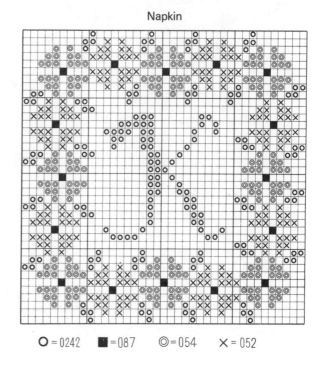

Edging (crochet with picots)

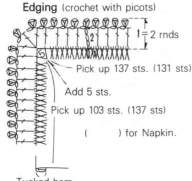

Pick up 137 sts. (131 sts)

Add 5 sts.

Pick up 103 sts. (137 sts)

( ) for Napkin.

Tucked hem

○ = 0242   ■ = 087   ◎ = 054   ✕ = 052

PILLOWS, shown on page 2

Materials for each: White Indian cloth (52 vertical and horizontal threads per 10 cm square) 85 cm by 47 cm/Inner Pillow 88 cm by 48 cm/37 cm-long zipper/Kapok 480 gr.

THREADS: DMC 6-strand embroidery floss:

Left pillow

3 skeins of Soft Pink (899); 1-1/2 skeins of Garnet Red (326).

Right pillow

3 skeins of Peacock Green (993); 1-1/2 skeins of Peacock Green (991).

Finished size: 44 cm by 41 cm.

Size of stitch: 1 square of design = 1 square mesh of fabric.

Directions: Use 3 strands of floss throughout. Find the center point of the embroidery area, and work on shifting the design from one corner to another. Put zipper on, then fold with right sides facing to then machine stitch. Put stuffed inner pillow in the embroidered pillow.

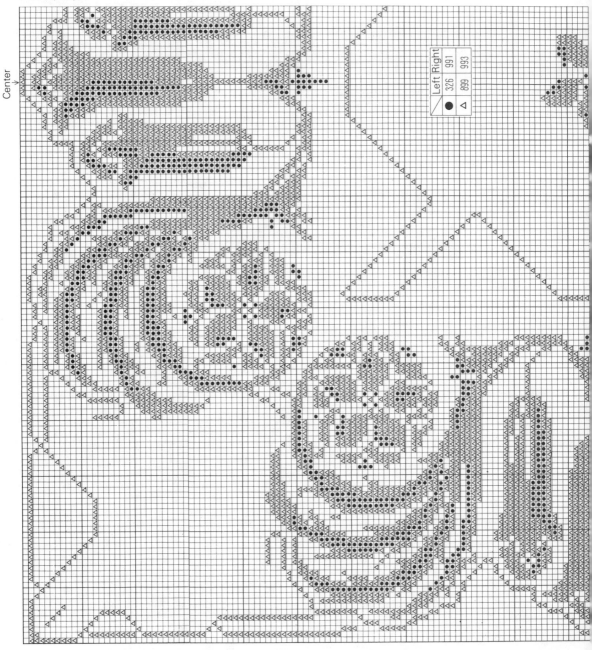

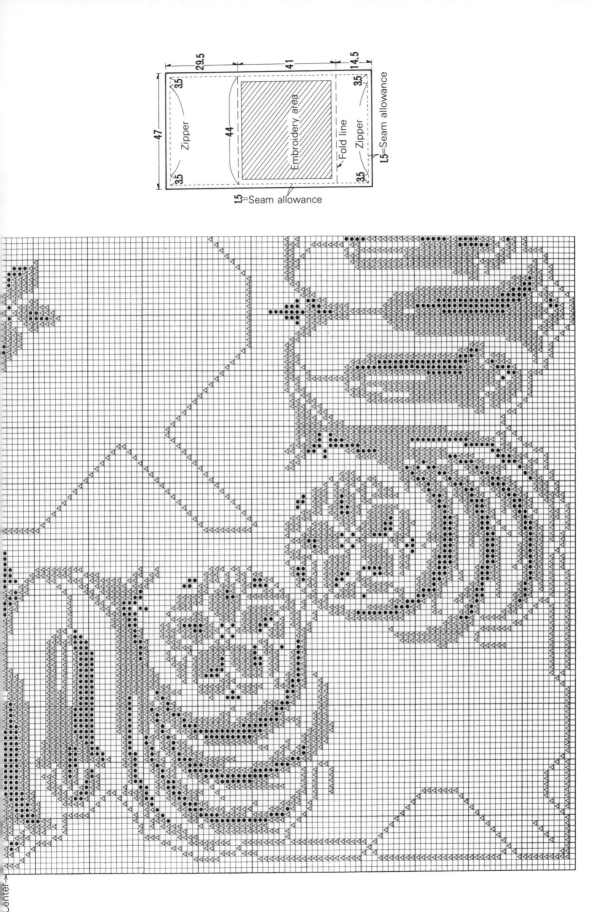

TABLECLOTH, shown on page 1

Materials: Beige Flat Linen cloth (80 vertical and horizontal threads per 10 cm square) 135.5 cm by 133.5 cm.
THREADS: DMC 6-strand embroidery floss: 17 skeins of Dark Brown (3033); 16 skeins of Flame Red (606); 14 skeins of Canary Yellow (971); 11 skeins of Tangerine Yellow (740); 8 skeins each of Geranium Red (982), Indigo (336); 4 skeins each of Canary Yellow (973), Umber Gold (977); 3 skeins each of Indigo (311), Peacock Green (992), Brilliant Green (701); 2 skeins each of Peacock Green (991), Fire Red (947), Geranium Red (754), Buttercup Yellow (444); 1 skein each of Emerald Green (911), Peacock Green (993), Turkey Red (321), Poppy (666), Parma Violet (208) and Brilliant Green (704).
Finished size: 127.5 cm by 125.5 cm.

Directions: Use 6 strands of floss throughout. 4-thread square is counted for each stitch in the chart. Find the centr point of the fabric, and count down the stitches to find the embroidery area. How to make the drawn work on center and hems are explained in the chart. Before draw threads on hems, finish the corners (mitered).

⊗ =311
I =973
● =321
✗ =444
◉ =704
S =740
V =991
∥ =992
— =993
O =947
T =701
X =336
P =892
C =971
■ =606
ℓ =754
∅ =208
⊤ =666
△ =977
7 =911

ㄴㄴ =971
Open-Buttonhole St.

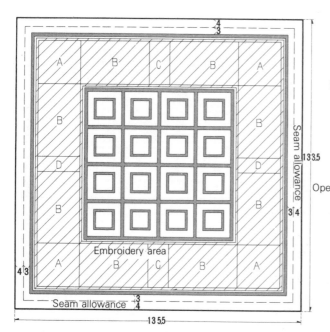

Embroidery area

Seam allowance

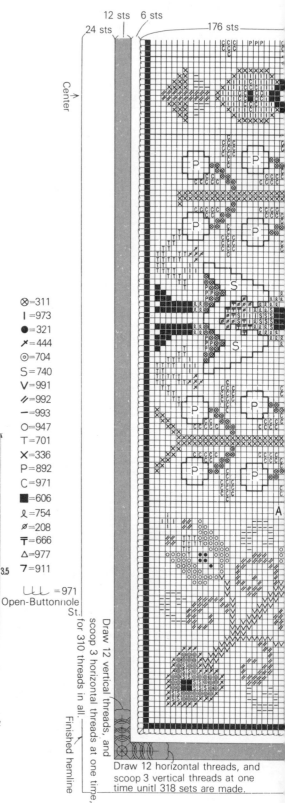

12 sts 6 sts
24 sts
176 sts
Center

Draw 12 vertical threads, and scoop 3 horizontal threads at one time, for 310 threads in all.
Finished hemline

Draw 12 horizontal threads, and scoop 3 vertical threads at one time unitl 318 sets are made.

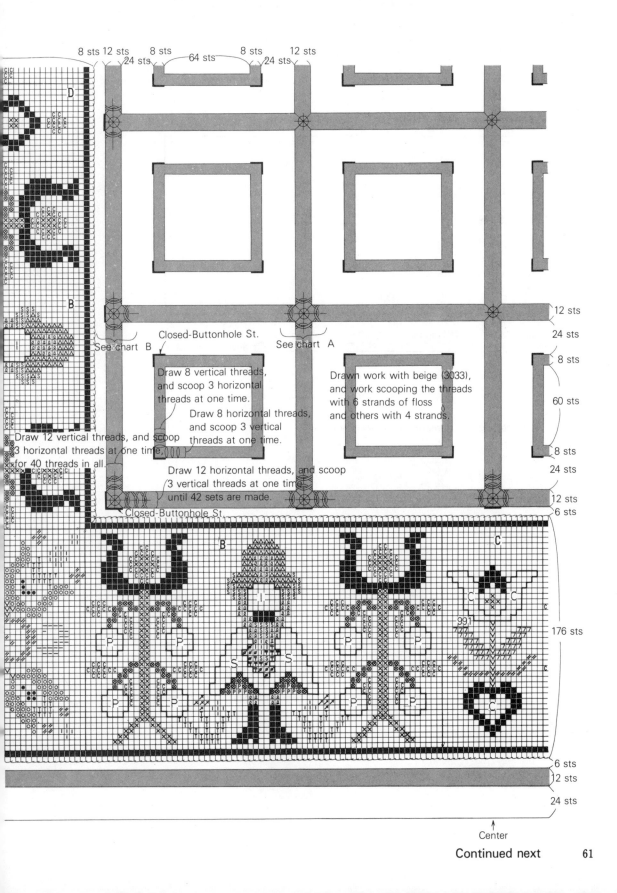

8 sts 12 sts   8 sts   64 sts   8 sts   12 sts
24 sts   24 sts

12 sts

24 sts

8 sts

60 sts

8 sts

24 sts

12 sts
6 sts

Closed-Buttonhole St.
See chart B   See chart A

Draw 8 vertical threads, and scoop 3 horizontal threads at one time.

Draw 8 horizontal threads, and scoop 3 vertical threads at one time.

Drawn work with beige (3033), and work scooping the threads with 6 strands of floss and others with 4 strands.

Draw 12 vertical threads, and scoop 3 horizontal threads at one time, for 40 threads in all.

Draw 12 horizontal threads, and scoop 3 vertical threads at one time, until 42 sets are made.

Closed-Buttonhole St.

176 sts

6 sts

12 sts

24 sts

↑
Center

Continued next   61

PILLOWS, shown on page 3

Materials: Beige Indian cloth (51 vertical and horizontal threads per 10cm square) 56.5cm by 99cm/Inner Pillow, stuffed with 650gr kapok 50.5cm by 99cm/36cm-long zipper.
THREADS: DMC 6-strand embroidery floss:

Top Pillow
15 skeins of Geranium Red (817); 4 skeins of Golden Yellow (783).
Bottom Pillow
15 skeins of Indigo (311); 4 skeins of Golden Yellow (783).

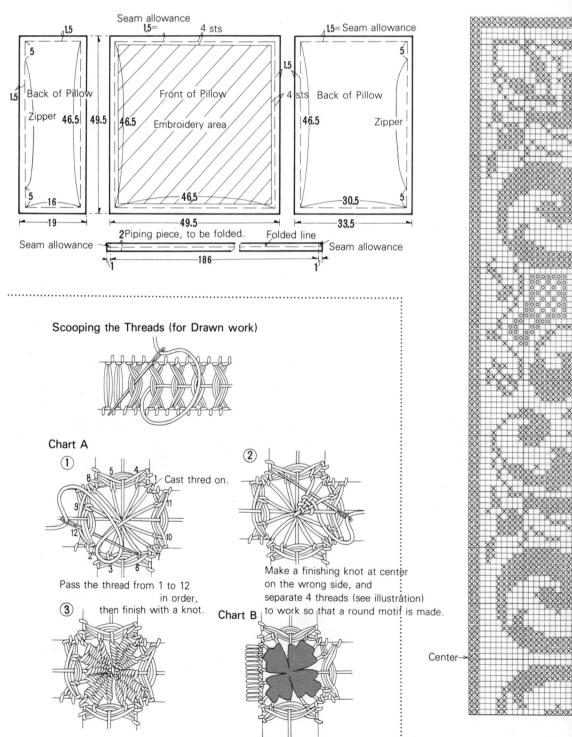

Scooping the Threads (for Drawn work)

Chart A

① Pass the thread from 1 to 12 in order, then finish with a knot.

② Make a finishing knot at center on the wrong side, and separate 4 threads (see illustration) to work so that a round motif is made.

③

Chart B

Center→

Finished size: 46.5 cm square.
Size of stitch: 1 square of design = 1 square mesh of fabric.
Directions: Use 3 strands of floss throughout. Find the center point of the embroidery area, and begin working there. Put on the zipper where indicated, then join front and back with the right sides facing, with piping piece inserted, to be then machined together. The piping piece is folded in two, and the folded side is shown on front. Put the inner pillow, stuffed with kapok, in the embroidered pillow.

Center

	Top pillow	Bottom pillow
X	817	311
O	783	783

PANEL, shown on page 5 (Top)

Materials: Beige Java cloth (36 vertical and horizontal threads per 10 cm square) 42 cm by 33 cm / Picture frame 37 cm by 28 cm (inside).

THREADS: DMC 6-strand embroidery floss: 3 skeins each of Parakeet Green (906), Saffron (727); 2-1/2 skeins of Avocado (470); 2 skeins each of Bronze Green (730), Yellow Green (733); 1-1/2 skeins each of Parakeet Green (904), Indigo (334), Forget-me-not Blue (827); 1 skein each of Parakeet Green (907, 905), Kelly Green (702, 701), Laurel Green (986), Copper Green (831), Coffee Brown (801), Nigger Brown (898), Myrtle Gray (927), Lemon Yellow (307), Light Yellow (3078); 1/2 skein each of Moss Green (935), Avocado (472, 471, 461), Peacock Green (993), Greenish Gray (597), Myrtle Gray (926), Beige (3047), Indigo (312), Ivy Green (500), Smoke Gray (822, 644), Umber (739), Terra-cotta (355), Garnet Red (309), Faded Pink (221), Antique Rose (223); small amount each of Pale Cream (746), Old Gold (677, 676), Faded Pink (225, 224), Dull Mauve (778), Geranium Red (350) and Umber (434).

Center →

							Center ↑		
キ = 701	∅ = 993	⊓ = 307	● = 500	▢ = 746	• = 831	■ = 935	I = 907	◎ = 730	P = 822	S = 677
⋗ = 905	∥ = 727	△ = 927	◐ = 986	✕ = 801	◓ = 471	T = 312	~ = 702	∧ = 644	# = 778	C = 350
V = 906	⊐ = 3078	+ = 3047	⊕ = 434	✳ = 898	✦ = 469	— = 827	A = 223	O = 355	人 = 225	Y = 676
⊗ = 904	⋉ = 224	⊙ = 472	‖ = 470	▲ = 926	φ = 733	= = 334	✕ = 597	L = 739	T̄ = 309	▼ = 221

Finished size: Same as the frame.
Directions: Use 6 strands of floss throughout. 1-thread square is counted for each stitch in the chart. Find the center point of the embroidery area, and begin working cross-stitches. Mount and frame.

PANEL, shown on page 4

Materials: Canvas cloth (70 vertical and horizontal threads per 10 cm square) 25 cm by 29.5 cm / Picture frame.
THREADS: DMC 6-strand embroidery floss: 2-1/2 skeins of Silver Gray (3072); 1 skein each of Drab (613), Army Green (3051); 1/2 skein each of Umber (437), Light Warm Tan (738), Beige Brown (842, 841), Dark Brown (3033), Myrtle Gray (928, 926), Antique Blue (931, 930), Smoke Gray (642, 640), Drab (611), Ivory (712), Pistachio Green (319, 318), Beaver Gray (648, 647), Army Green (3052), Green (3053), Almond Green (503), Copper Green (830), Khaki Green (3013, 3012, 3011), Old Gold (729), Seagull Gray (452), Faded Pink(221), Antique Rose (223); small amount each of Terra-cotta (356, 355), Myrtle Gray (928, 927, 924), Hazel-nut Brown (422, 420), Umber (436), Drab (610), Old Gold (680, 676), Beige (3045, 3023), Beige Brown (840), Faded Pink (224), Seagull Gray (451), Ivy Green (501), Almond Green (504, 502), Beaver Gray (646) and Ash Gray (762).
Finished size: As shown below.
Directions: Use 4 strands of floss througout. 1-thread square is counted for each stitch in the chart. Find the center point of the embroidery area, and work in half-cross-stitches. You may need professional help for framing.

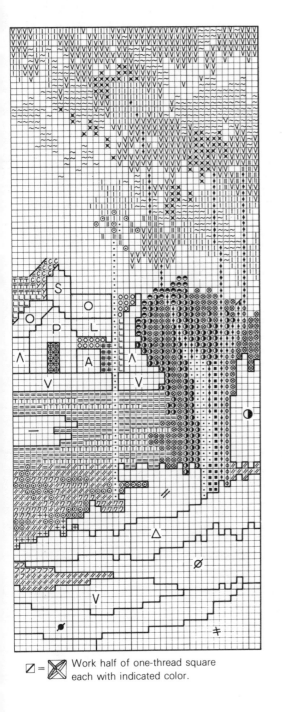

= Work half of one-thread square each with indicated color.

Finished Panel

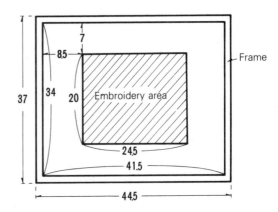

(Continued next.)

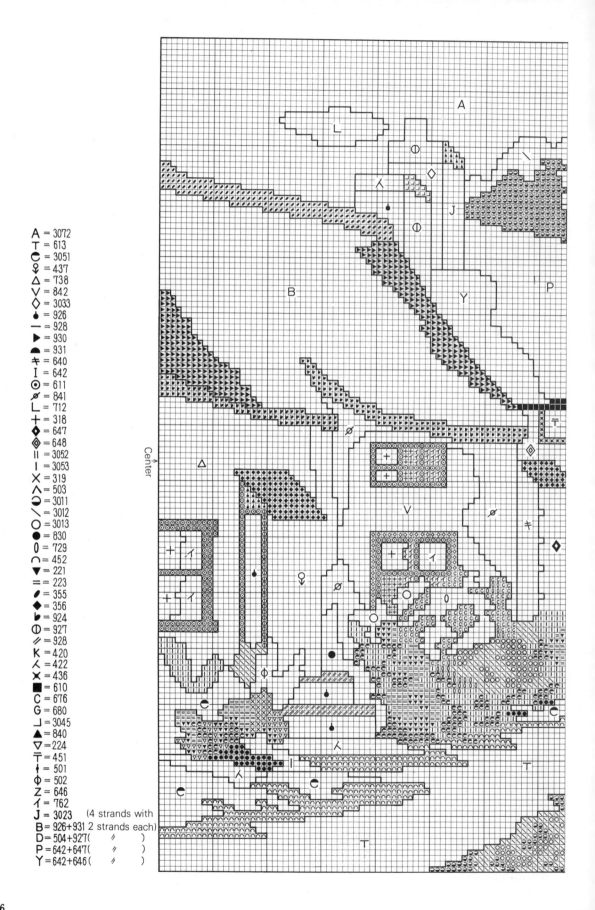

A = 3072
T = 613
C = 3051
♀ = 437
△ = 738
V = 842
◇ = 3033
• = 926
— = 928
▶ = 930
◣ = 931
ꝁ = 640
I = 642
⊙ = 611
∅ = 841
L = 712
+ = 318
◆ = 647
◈ = 648
|| = 3052
| = 3053
X = 319
∧ = 503
⊃ = 3011
╲ = 3012
O = 3013
● = 830
0 = 729
∩ = 452
▼ = 221
= = 223
🌑 = 355
◆ = 356
ь = 924
Φ = 927
// = 928
K = 420
人 = 422
✕ = 436
■ = 610
C = 676
G = 680
⌐ = 3045
▲ = 840
▽ = 224
〒 = 451
† = 501
Φ = 502
Z = 646
イ = 762
J = 3023   (4 strands with
B = 926+931 2 strands each)
D = 504+927 (//)
P = 642+647 (//)
Y = 642+646 (//)

Center

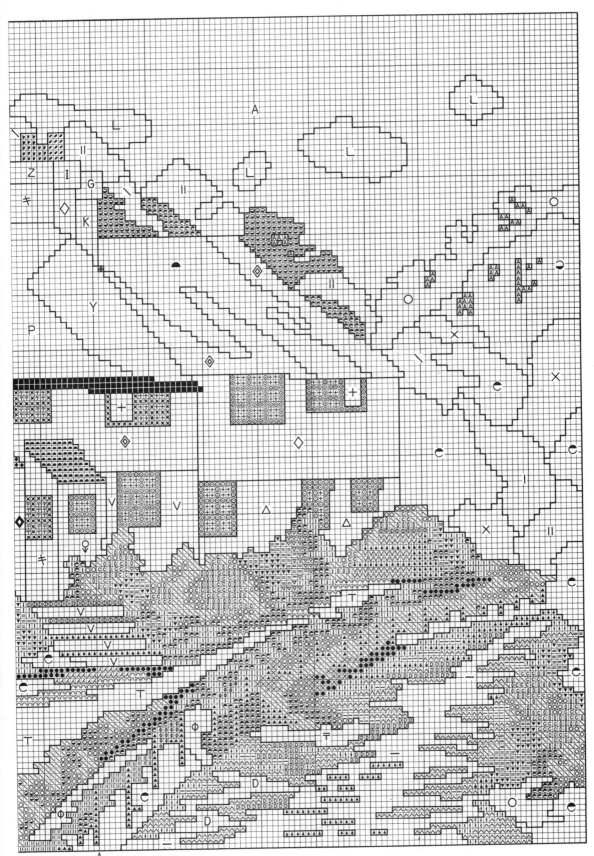

Center

PILLOWS, shown on page 5 (Bottom)

Materials: (for each) Beige Java cloth (36 vertical and horizontal threads per 10 cm square) 87 cm by 45 cm/Cotton fabric for Inner Pillow 90 cm by 46 cm/34 cm-long zipper/ 400 gr kapok.

THREADS: DMC 6-strand embroidery floss:

● = 300 (815)
O = 918 (304)
A = 920 (350)
B }
◇ } 922 (351)
C = 402 (352)
D }
X } 469 (469)
E = 912 (912)
F = 471 (471)
G = 937 (937)
• = 781 (347)
△ = 783 (3328)
H = 725 (761)
I = 726 (760)
J = 727 (761)
I = 644 (644)
λ = 642 (642)

Color number in parentheses are indicated for left pillow.

Center

Right pillow
1-1/2 skeins each of Red Brown (920), Saffron (726); 1 skein each of Mahogany (402, 300), Red Brown (922, 918), Golden Yellow (783, 781), Dark Yellow Gold (725), Saffron (727), Moss Green (937), Avocado (471, 479), Emerald Green (912), Smoke Gray (644); 1/2 skein of Smoke Gray (642).

Left pillow
1-1/2 skeins each of Geranium Red (350), Morocco Red (760); 1 skein each of Scarlet (815, 304), Coral (351), Geranium Red (352), Cardinal Red (347), Morocco Red (3328, 761), Moss Green (937), Avocado (471, 469), Emerald Green (912), Smoke Gray (644); 1/2 skein of Smoke Gray (642).

Finished size: 42 cm square.

Directions: Use 6 strands of floss througout. 1-thread square is counted for each stitch in the chart. Find center point of the embroidery area, and work cross-stitches from that point. Sew in zipper. Join front and back of the pillow with right sides facing, and machine stitch around. Put in the inner pillow.

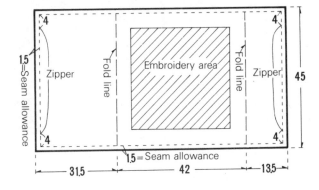

SMALL PICTURE IN FRAME, shown on page 6

Materials: Canvas cloth (80 vertical and horizontal threads per 10 cm square) 28 cm by 21.5 cm / Picture frame 23 cm by 16.5 cm (inside).

THREADS: DMC 6-strand embroidery floss: 3 skeins of Black (310); 1/2 skein each of white, Jade Green (943), Peacock Green (992, 991), Kelly Green (702, 701), Ivory (704), Parakeet Green (907, 906), Yellow Green (733), Peacock Blue (519, 518, 517), Sky Blue (747), Turquoise (598), Electric Blue (996), Cornflower Blue (792, 791), Sévres Blue (799, 798), Baby Blue (800), Indigo (311), Saffron (727), Dark Yellow Orange (742), Canary Yellow (973, 972, 971), Medium Yellow Orange (743), Dark Red Orange (900), Fire Red (946), Ash Gray (415, 318), Lilac (210), Scarlet (3041), Indian Red (3042), Red Brown (920), Rust Red (921), Beige (3046, 3045), Umber Gold (976), Old Gold (3350, 729, 680, 676), Umber (435), Garnet Red (335, 309), Soft Pink (899), Fuschia Pink (604, 603, 602, 601, 600), Cerise (605), Raspberry Red (3688, 3687), Dull Mauve (316, 315), Faded Pink (221), Antique Rose (223); small amount each of Kelly Green (703), Emerald Green (913), Army Green (3052), Peacock Blue (806), Lemon Yellow (307), Dark Yellow Gold (725), Myrtle Gray (927, 926), Episcopal Purple (915), Plum (554) and Hot Pink (956). Anchor 6-strand embroidery floss: 1/2 skein each of Dark Red Orange (333), Jade Green (118), Peacock Green (187, 186), Red Brown (326)

Finished size: Same as the frame.

Directions: Use 3 strands of floss throughout. 1-thread square is counted for each stitch in the chart. Find the center point of the embroidery area, and begin working in half-cross-stitches. Mount and frame.

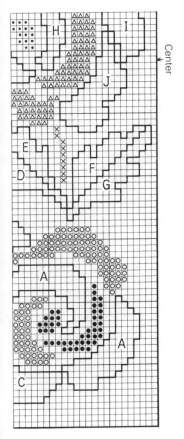

(Continued next.)

Center →

↑
Center

• = White
● = 943
▲ = 991
✍ = 992
V = 701
△ = 702
▲ = 703
⋋ = 704
⊢ = 906
⊕ = 907
~ = 913
↙ = 3052
✛ = 733
✳ = 517
✕ = 518
H = 519
I = 747
Z = 598
Z = 806
⊖ = 996
◐ = 791
⬎ = 792
# = 798
C = 799
╲ = 800
✕ = 311
↗ = 307
⊖ = 725
⊕ = 727
◉ = 742
◎ = 743
O = 972
⅋ = 973
◓ = 900
2 = 946
⊠ = 971
Y = 318
S = 415
△ = 926
✳ = 927
◆ = 915
フ = 210
✏ = 554
K = 3041
N = 3042
◣ = 920
☐ = 921
// = 3045
/ = 3046
E = 976
Ⅲ = 680
✕ = 729
‖ = 676
✳ = 435
◑ = 309
⊗ = 335
◇ = 899
◇ = 600
⬐ = 601
⬦ = 602
L = 603
↗ = 604
P = 605
⅊ = 3687
〒 = 3688
α = 956
✕ = 3350
✕ = 315
+ = 316
◤ = 221
◈ = 223
△ = 0333
Π = 0188
J = 0187
≶ = 0186
◪ = 0326

※ Fill with black for open space.

(Continued next.)

SMALL WALL HANGING, shown on page 8 (Left)

Materials: Beige Java cloth (60 vertical and horizontal threads per 10 cm square) 61 cm by 24 cm/Metal ends.

THREADS: DMC 6-strand embroidery floss: 1 skein each of Khaki Green (3011), Army Green (3051), White; 1/2 skein each of Coffee Brown (801), Umber (437, 434), Golden Yellow (783), Khaki Green (3012), Brown (3064), Ivy Green (500), Pistachio Green (320), Bronze Green (730), Geranium red (349), Light Red Orange (947), Cardinal Red (347), Soft Pink (819, 818), Light Yellow Orange (744), Canary Yellow (972, 793); small amount each of Indigo (823), Royal Blue (797).

Finished size: 54 cm lengthwise, 10 cm widthwise, excluding metal ends.

Directions: Find embroidery area, and begin working cross-stitches (with 3 strands of floss) and holbein stitches (double strands of floss). See illustration for finishing.

Holbein (972)

Holbein (818)

Holbein (434)

Center

⊗ = 783	◐ = 500	◎ = 3051
■ = 823	◓ = 320	✕ = 3012
▾ = 797	● = 349	✔ = 972
⌀ = 793	◢ = 744	• = White
⋰ = 437	✳ = 434	✖ = 3011
⊙ = 801	+ = 730	I = 3064
I = 819	▲ = 347	
○ = 947	△ = 818	

Center

Holbein
(801)

Holbein
(801)

(Continued before.)

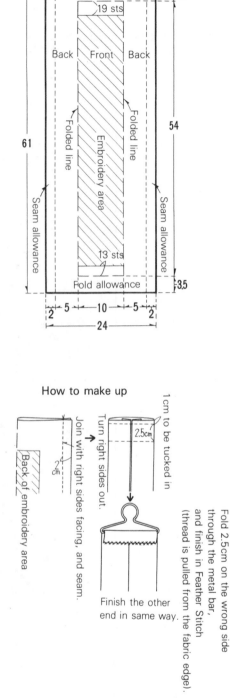

35

19 sts

Back   Front   Back

Folded line

Folded line

Embroidery area

54

61

Seam allowance

Seam allowance

13 sts

Fold allowance

35

2 — 5 — 10 — 5 — 2

24

How to make up

Back of embroidery area

Join with right sides facing, and seam.

2 cm

Turn right sides out.

1cm to be tucked in

2.5cm

Fold 2.5cm on the wrong side through the metal bar, and finish in Feather Stitch (thread is pulled from the fabric edge).

Finish the other end in same way.

PANEL, shown on page 7 (Bottom)

Materials: Beige Indian cloth (51 vertical and horizontal threads per 10 cm square) 40.5 cm by 38.5 cm/Picture frame.
THREADS: DMC 6-strand embroidery floss: 1-1/2 skeins each of Moss Green (937), Plum (552); 1 skein each of Khaki Green (3011), Moss Green (469); 1/2 skein each of Avocado (472), Pistachio Green (367, 320), Khaki Green (3013, 3012), Scarlet (902), Dark Lilac (550), Fuschia-Pink (604, 603, 601, 600), Hot Pink (957), Dark Yellow Orange (742), Lemon Yellow (307), Saffron

Center

■ = 937
I = 367
✗ = 320
+ = 504
— = 3011
• = 3012
O = 3013
✗ = 472
◒ = 902
▼ = 550
● = 553
⊙ = 554
◢ = 600
T = 601
⟍ = 603
S = 604
∅ = 957
⊗ = 742
✗ = 307
∧ = 726
△ = 469
// = 552
L = 553
L⌐ = 3012
 ⌐ (Holbein)

Center

74

(726), Plum (553), small amount each of Almond Green (504), Plum (554).
Finished size: As shown on right.
Directions: Use 3 strands of floss throughout. 1-thread square is counted for each stitch in the chart. Find the center point of the embroidery area, and begin working cross-stitches.

Finished diagram

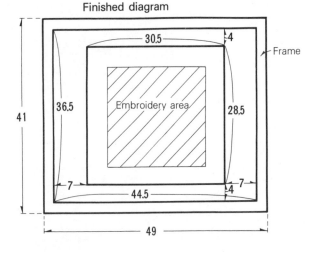

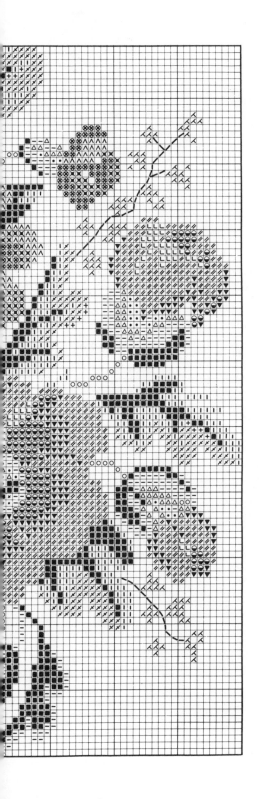

PANEL, shown on page 8 (Right)

Materials: Linen Oxford cloth (80 vertical and 90 horizontal threads per 10 cm square) 42.5 cm by 32.5 cm / Picture frame (illustrated).
THREADS: DMC 6-strand embroidery floss: 1 skein each of Parakeet Green (907, 905), Pistachio Green (368), Kelly Green (701), Watermelon Pink (894); 1/2 skein each of Laurel Green (987), Almond Green (503), Terra-cotta (356), Umber (433), Cornflower Blue (792), Dark Yellow Orange (742), Saffron (726), Garnet Red (309), Magenta Rose (963, 961); small amount each of Umber (435), Raspberry Red (3685) and Umber Gold (977). Anchor 6-strand embroidery floss: 1/2 skein each of Cornflower Blue (119, 118).
Finished size: Illustrated.
Size of stitch: 1 square of design = 1 square mesh of fabric.
Directions: Find the center point of the embroidery area, and begin working cross-stitches with 3 strands of floss, and holbein sttiches with double strands of floss. Mount and frame.

(Continued next.)

10 cm = 90 sts

10 cm = 80 sts

Center

Center

ℓ =701　Z =907　∴=905　❧=963　O=894　△=309　◉=961　●=3685　◀=742　==726　∿∿=435
▲=433　◢=977　✗=356　✕=792　Ⅱ=0119　V=0118　X=368　■=987　I=503
‒‒=907 ⎫
　　　　⎬ Holbein
----=701 ⎭

TABLE RUNNER & PILLOWS, shown on page 12

Materials: Beige Java cloth (36 vertical and horizontal threads per 10 cm square) 51 cm by 94 cm for Runner, and 89 cm by 46 cm for each Pillow/Cotton fabric for inner pillows 47 cm by 92 cm for each/2 40 cm-long zippers/600 gr kapok for each inner pillow.

THREADS: DMC 6-strand embroidery floss:
Table runner
3-1/2 skeins of Myrtle Gray (926); 3 skeins of Raspberry Red (3689); 1 skein of Brilliant Green (703); 1/2 skein of Canary Yellow (973).
Pillow [For one pillow]
2 skeins each of Myrtle Gray (926), Raspberry Red (3687); 1/2 skein each of Brilliant Green (703), Canary Yellow (973).

Finished size: Runner 94 cm by 43 cm, Pillows 43 cm square.

Directions: 1-thread square is counted for each stitch in the chart. Use 4 strands of floss. Find center point of the embroidery area of each piece, and begin from that point. Longer sides of Runner are finished in hem trimming (with the edge folded twice then sew up with hand), and shorter sides with self-fringes. Inner pillows, stuffed with kapok.

Table runner

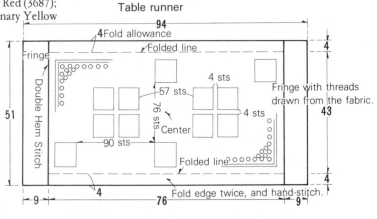

Patterns for table runner

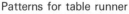

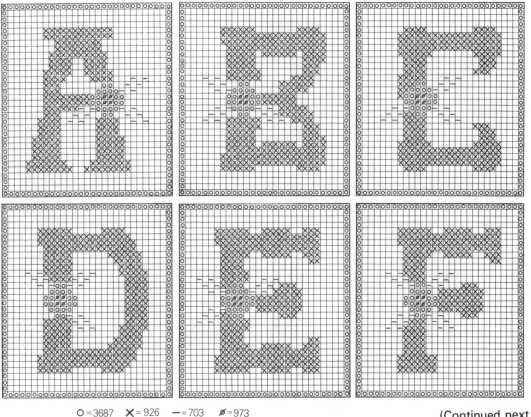

O = 3687   X = 926   — = 703   ∅ = 973

(Continued next.)

Patterns for table runner

Center

Pillow

89

1.5
1.5
1.5
46
Seam allowance
Zipper
Folded line
Embroidery area
Center
Folded line
Zipper
1.5
1.5
1.5
1.5
15
43
28
1.5
1.5

Mitered corner

Tuck the corner in, and sew.

4 cm

Right pillow   Center

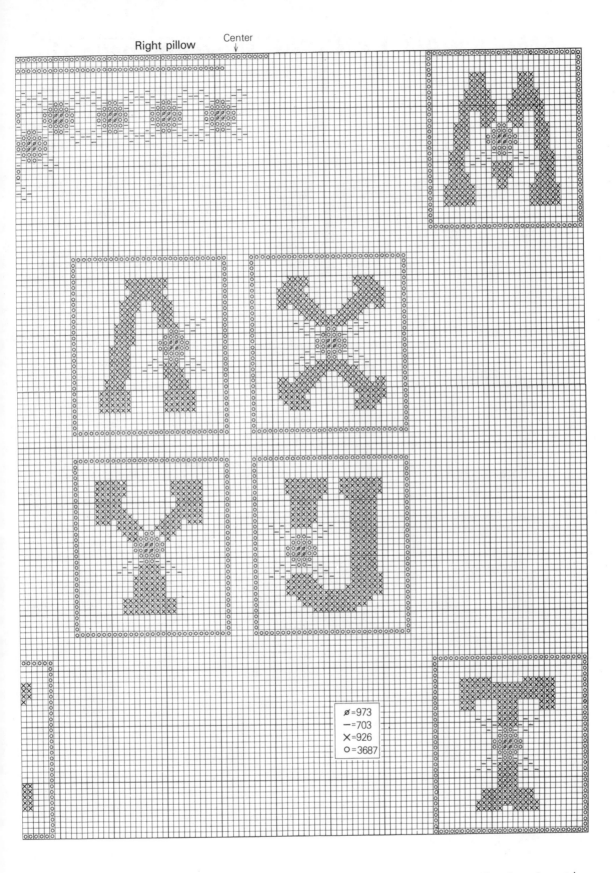

Ø =973
— =703
X =926
O =3687

(Continued next.)

SMALL WALL HANGING, shown on page 11

Materials: Black Aida cloth (35 vertical and horizontal threads per 10 cm square) 50 cm by 44 cm/Black unwoven textile with the wrong side glued (available at speciality shop) 46 cm by 36 cm/Heavyweight cardboard 34 cm length and 2 cm width/1.5 cm-wide Black bias strip 170 cm/Small amount of yarn (for hanging)/Glue.

THREADS: DMC 6-strand embroidery floss: 3 skeins of Geranium Red (350); 2-1/2 skeins each of Red Brown (920), Umber Gold (976); 2 skeins each of Rust Red (918), Brilliant Red (666); 1-1/2 skeins each of Scarlet (304), Geranium Red (817), Flame Red (606); small amount each of Umber (436), Umber Gold (977), Scarlet (814).

Finished size: 46 cm by 36 cm.

Size of stitch: 1 square of design = 1 square mesh of fabric.

Directions: Find the embroidery area in the fabric, and work cross-stitches. Use 6 strands of floss throughout. Place the unwoven textile over the wrong side of the embroidered piece, and finish as shown below. Choose strong yarn for hanging strings.

Patterns for left pillow

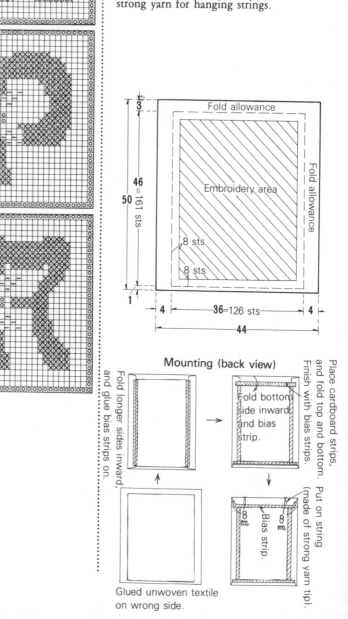

80

= =817   A =666   ‖ =304   Z =814   E =976   ✕ =918

✍ =606   ℓ =920   ▲ =350   ✐ =977   ☻ =436

Materials: Canvas cloth (50 vertical and horizontal threads per 10 cm square) 39 cm by 31.5 cm/Picture frame.

I = 471	# = 818	B = 225	⊐ = 632
P = 3047	◢ = Black	⊖ = 3685	✕ = 3347
T = 3045	O = 996	☸ = 815	⊢ = 704
✗ = 676	7 = White	∧ = 304	⊼ = 828
△ = 469	+ = 762	▗ = 946	‖ = 807
∅ = 726	● = 415	Z = 745	▲ = 089
✗ = 725	Y = 605	C = 224	◑ = 088
∥ = 3022	⊙ = 603	E = 801	◐ = 086
■ = 844	⊗ = 604	∡ = 223	V = 085
✚ = 367	⊤ = 776	⊖ = 919	
L = 813	= = 912	H = 677	
⟋ = 826	⟍ = 326	⊠ = 500	
O = 335	A = 987	⊥ = 502	
◎ = 309	◖ = 319	✗ = 209	
• = 743	X = 3346	⟨ = 3345	
ℓ = 320	R = 613	⌃ = 435	
✳ = 434	S = 739	▼ = 838	
~ = 819	— = 800	ⱽ = 975	

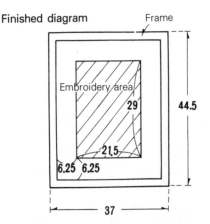

Finished diagram — Frame

Embroidery area

29

44.5

21.5

6.25 6.25

37

THREADS: DMC 6-strand embroidery floss: 4 skeins of Peacock Blue (807); 2-1/2 skeins each of Baby Blue (800), Avocado (471), Beige (3045); 1 skein each of White, Cerise (605), Beige (3022), Old Gold (676), Emerald Green (912); 1/2 skein each of Beige (3047), Saffron (726), Dark Yellow Gold (725), Beaver Gray (844), Garnet Red (335), Pistachio Green (320, 319), Fuschia Pink (604, 603), Drab (613), Umber (739, 434), Laurel Green (987), Scarab Green (3347, 3346, 3345), Ivy Green (500), Almond Green (502), Beige Brown (838), Ivory (704); small amount each of Forget-me-not Blue (828, 826, 813), Medium Yellow Orange (743), Soft Pink (819, 818, 776), Royal Blue (996), Garnet Red (326, 309), Faded Pink (225, 224), Raspberry Red (3685), Scarlet (815, 304), Fire Red (946), Pale Yellow Orange (745), Antique Rose (223), Coffee Brown (801), Red Brown (919), Old Gold (677), Parma Violet (209), Ash Gray (762, 415), Moss Green (469), Pistachio Green (367), Cinnamon Orange (975), Chocolate (632) and Umber (435).
Anchor 6-strand embroidery floss: 2 skeins each of Episcopal Purple (88), Raspberry Red (86); 1 skein each of Episcopal Purple (89), Raspberry Red (85).
Finished size: Illustrated.
Directions: Use 6 strands of floss. Find the center point of the embroidery area, and work half-cross-stitches throughout. 1-thread square is coutned for each stitch in the chart. You may need professional help for finished panel.

TABLE RUNNER, shown on page 10

Materials: Beige Java cloth (50 vertical and horizontal threads per 10 cm square) 55 cm by 204 cm.
THREADS: DMC 6-strand embroidery floss: 7 skeins of Umber (436); 6 skeins of Umber (437), 5-1/2 skeins each of Geranium Pink (892, 891); 4 skeins each of Dark Yellow Orange (742), Medium Yellow Orange (743); 1-1/2 skeins each of Scarab Green (3347, 3346), 1 skein each of Tangerine Yellow (740), Moss Green (966),

Scarab Green (3348); 1/2 skein each of Geranium Red (350), Terra-cotta (356), Flame Red (608) and Fire Red (946).
Finished size: 43 cm by 192 cm.
Directions: 1-thread square is counted for each stitch in the chart. Find the embroidery area, and work with 4 strands of floss throughout. To finish, hem around four sides (with the corners mitered).

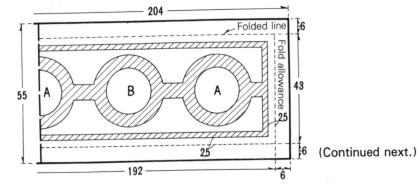

204

Folded line 6

Fold allowance

55 A B A 43

25

192 6

25 6

(Continued next.)

	A	B
○	892	742
✕	966	3348
∅	740	356
⊕	350	946
●	891	743
V	608	740
✕	3347	
△	3346	
=	436	
−	437	

A

TABLE RUNNER, shown on page 16 (Top)

Materials: White Java cloth (36 vertical and horizontal threads per 10 cm square) 89 cm by 50 cm.

THREADS: DMC 6-strand embroidery floss: 10 skeins of Cranberry Red (321); 7-1/2 skeins of Episcopal Purple (917); 3-1/2 skeins of Flame Red (608).

Finished size: 81 cm by 42 cm.

Size of stitch: 1 square of design = 1 square mesh of fabric.

Directions: Use 6 strands of floss throughout. Find the center point of the embroidery area, and begin from that point. To finish, fold in all edges (twice) and hand-stitch scooping the threads cast on the wrong side. Finish the corners as illustrated below.

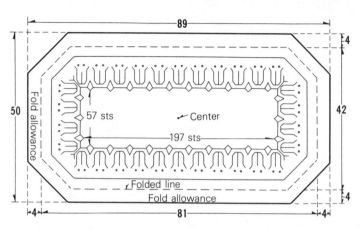

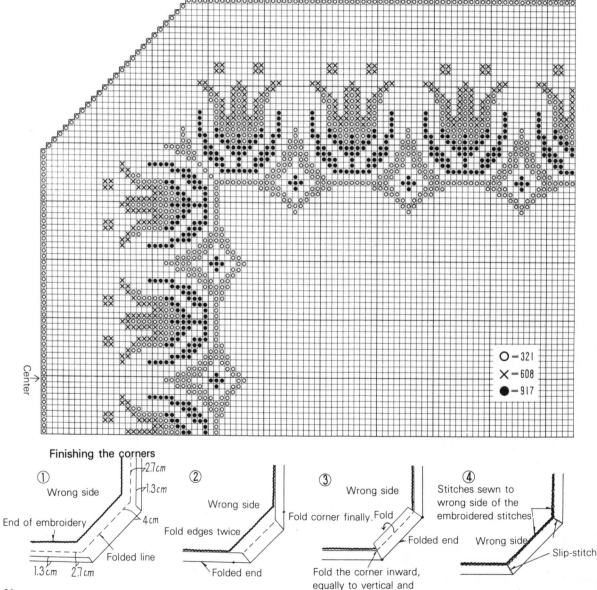

O = 321
X = 608
● = 917

Finishing the corners

① Wrong side
End of embroidery
2.7 cm
1.3 cm
4 cm
Folded line
1.3 cm   2.7 cm

② Wrong side
Fold edges twice
Folded end

③ Wrong side
Fold corner finally. Fold
Folded end
Fold the corner inward, equally to vertical and horizontal measurement.

④ Stitches sewn to wrong side of the embroidered stitches
Wrong side
Slip-stitch

TABLE RUNNER, shown on page 16 (Bottom)

Materials: Light beige Java cloth (36 vertical and horizontal threads per 10 cm square) 90 cm by 50 cm.

THREADS: DMC 6-strand embroidery floss: 3 skeins each of Geranium Red (350), Brilliant Green (701); 2 skeins each of Red Brown (922), Coffee Brown (938), Moss Green (470); 1 skein of Canary Yellow (972).

Finished size: 75 cm by 35 cm.

Size of stitch: 1 square of design = 1 square mesh of fabric.

Directions: Find the embroidery area, and work with 6 strands of floss throughout, starting from the center point. To finish, fold in all edges twice, and hand-stitch (with the corners mitered).

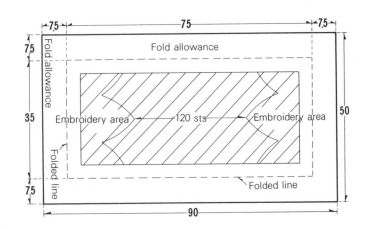

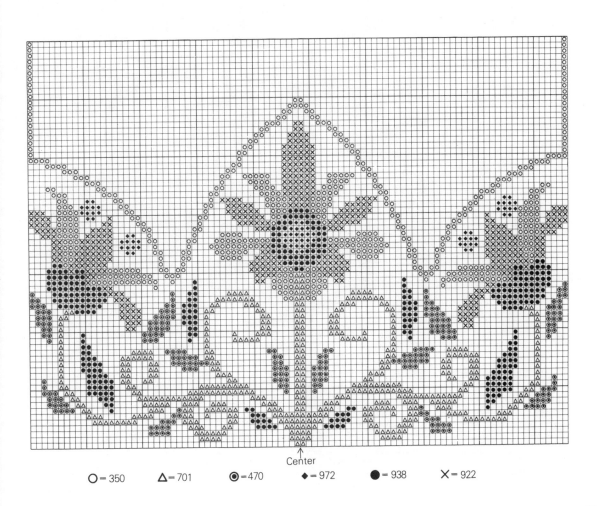

Center

O = 350   △ = 701   ◉ = 470   ◆ = 972   ● = 938   X = 922

TABLECLOTH, shown on page 14

Materials: Beige Java cloth (52 vertical and horizontal threads per 10 cm square) 105 cm by 134 cm/Loosely twisted floss in beige (#20) 20 gr.

THREADS: DMC 6-strand embroidery floss: 6 skeins of Emerald Green (912); 5 skeins of Emerald Green (954); 3 skeins each of Light Yellow Orange (744), Khaki Green (3013), Lilac (210, 208); 2 skeins each of Peacock Blue (519), Sky Blue (747), Emerald Green (911), Magenta Rose (962, 961), Soft Pink (3326), Old Gold (676); 1 skein each of Peacock Blue (518), Khaki Green (3012); 1/2 skein each of Dark Yellow Gold (725), Parma Violet (209). DMC cotton thread No. 30: 20 gr of beige.

Finished size: 133.5 cm by 104.5 cm.

Size of stitch: 1 square of design = 1 square mesh of fabric.

⊙ = 911	L = 209	✕ = 962	▲ = 3012
◎ = 912	⊕ = 747	∥ = 961	△ = 3013
○ = 954	⊖ = 518	✖ = 725	
+ = 210	◇ = 519	✦ = 676	
☐ = 208	‖ = 3326	— = 744	

Directions: Find each embroidery area according to the chart. Use 3 strands of floss throughout. To finish, work edging (of crochet) so that folded edge is wrapped.

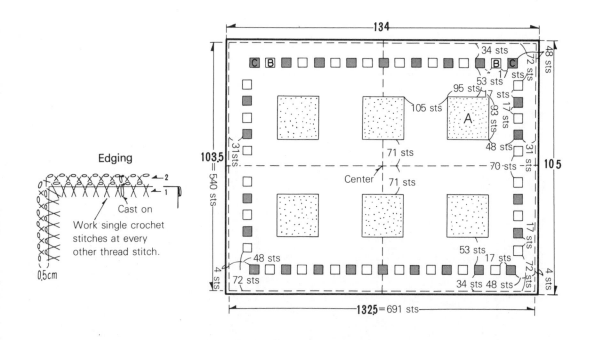

Edging

X

2

1

Cast on

Work single crochet
stitches at every
other thread stitch.

0.5cm

134

34 sts

48 sts
72 sts

17 sts

53 sts

17 sts

95 sts

105 sts

A

93 sts

48 sts

31 sts
17 sts

103.5
= 540 sts

31 sts

71 sts

70 sts

105

Center

71 sts

17 sts

53 sts

17 sts
72 sts

48 sts

72 sts

34 sts 48 sts

4 sts

4 sts

132.5 = 691 sts

WALL HANGINGS, shown on page 15

Materials for one: Beige Aida cloth (35 vertical and horizontal threads per 10 cm square) 38 cm by 37.5 cm/Cotton fabric for lining 33.5 cm by 37.5 cm.
THREADS: Top
Anchor 6-strand embroidery floss: 2 skeins of Turquoise (185); 1 skein each of Cornflower Blue (118, 117), Garnet Red (29), Brilliant Green (227), Cerise (63), Episcopal Purple (88), Avocado (278), Almond Green (208), Cornflower Blue (137); 1/2 skein each of Fushcia Pink (62), Geranium Red (11), Kelly Green (329), Scarab Green (254); small amount each of Light Red Orange (329), Jade Green (188), Peacock Green (187), White, Dark Yellow Gold (306), Avocado (253), Ash Gray (400).

DMC 6-strand embroidery floss: 5 skeins of Copper Green (831); 2-1/2 skeins of Army Green (3051); 1 skein each of Yellow Green (734), Copper Green (830); 1/2 skein of Golden Green (580).
Bottom
Anchor 6-strand embroidery floss: 2 skeins each of Cornflower Blue (118), Episcopal Purple (88); 1-1/2 skeins of Peacock Green (187); 1 skein each of Emerald Green (204), Bronze Green (855), Parma Violet (108), Fuschia Pink (63), Garnet Red (57), Umber (358), Turquoise (185); 1/2 skein each of Kelly Green (329, 228, 214), Parakeet Green (254), Dark Yellow Gold (306),

Cutting diagram

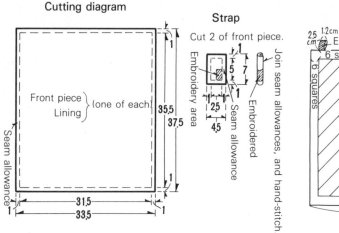

Front piece
Lining } (one of each)

35.5

37.5

Seam allowance

Seam allowance

31.5

33.5

1

Strap

Cut 2 of front piece.

Embroidery area

5

7

1

25

4.5

Embroidered

Seam allowance

Join seam allowances, and hand-stitch.

Finished diagram

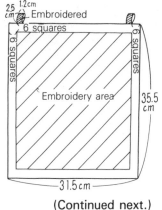

2.5
cm

1.2cm
Embroidered

6 squares

6 squares

6 squares

Embroidery area

35.5
cm

31.5cm

(Continued next.)

89

Kelly Green (328), Cornflower Blue (136); small amount each of Jade Green (188), Kelly Green (227), White. DMC 6-strand embroidery floss: 2-1/2 skeins of Army Green (3051); 1-1/2 skeins of Copper Green (831); 1 skein of Yellow Green (634).

Finished size: Illustrated.

Directions: 1-thread square is counted for each stitch in teh chart. Find the center point of the embroidery, and work with 6 strands of floss. The straps are cross-stitched also. To finish, join the embroidered piece with the lin-ing, with the right sides facing, and machine-stitch around, leaving the top edge unstitched (to be then finished with hand after inserting straps.)

▲ =0118	╱ =0254	˅ =088	├ =062	⬤ =0187	△ =831	✗ =580	Strap
— =0188	∅ =029	• =0185	◎ =011	‹ =0253	⊤ =734	⌐ =0400 (Holbein)	
⊗ =0329	L =0227	∥ =0117	◇ =White	⊖ =0208	⬤ =830		
◀ =0239	I =063	T =0278	✖ =0306	ø =0137	✕ =3051		

90

Bottom

Center →

↑ Center

Symbol	Value	Symbol	Value	Symbol	Value	Symbol	Value	Symbol	Value
▲	=0118	∨	=088	✔	=0228	L	=0238	O	=0187
∥	=0108	●	=0358	╱	=831				
—	=0188	T̄	=0204	⊖	=0254	╳	=0239	◇	=White
I	=063	•	=0185	△	=734				
⊕	=0227	✦	=0214	✖	=03C6	∅	=0136	⊢	=057
∧	=0855	╳	=3051						

Strap

WALL POCKETS, shown on page 22

Materials: Beige Java cloth (50 vertical and horizontal threads per 10 cm square) 81 cm by 52.5 cm / Cotton fabric for lining 64.5 cm by 12 cm / Fusible unwoven textile (if available) 58.5 cm by 12.5 cm / Wooden bar of 1 cm-diameter 28 cm.
THREADS: DMC 6-strand embroidery floss: 2 skeins of Umber (434); 1-1/2 skeins of Peacock Blue (518); 1 skein each of Cinnamon Orange (975), Emerald Green (911), Scarlet (304), Parakeet Green (906); 1/2 skein each of

Canary Yellow (970), Rosy Flesh (950), Umber Gold (976), Scarab Green (3346), Sévres Blue (799), Royal Blue (797); small amount each of Black (310), Respberry Red (3689).
Finished size: 54 cm by 25 cm (Pocketed hanging only).
Directions: 1-thread square is counted for each stitch in the chart. Use 4 strands of floss throughout. Follow charts A, B and C for cross-ctitching. Put the em-

broidered pieces on each pocket. Make the pockets with lining, and sew them on the panel piece. Pass the wooden bar through on top. Make a cord as illustrated.

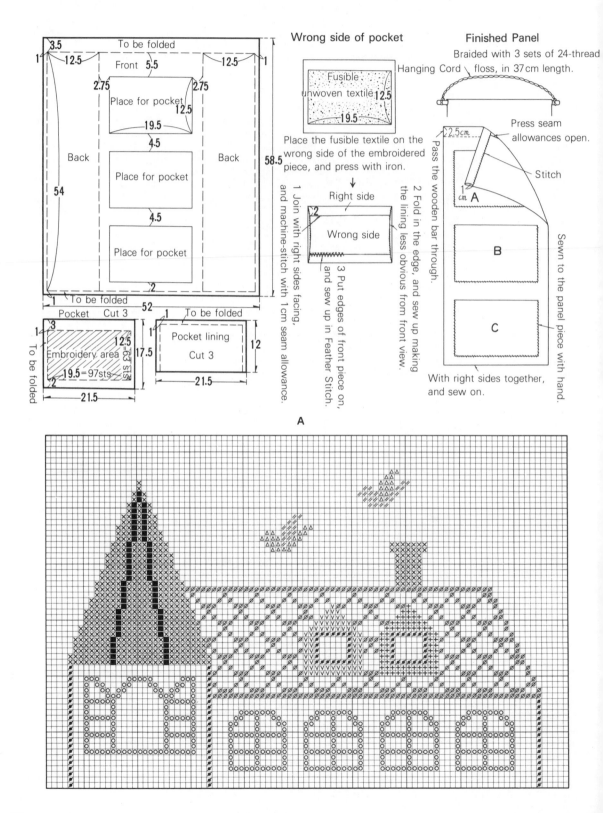

3.5
To be folded
1
12.5
Front 5.5
12.5
1
2.75
2.75
Place for pocket
12.5
19.5
4.5
Back
Back
Place for pocket
54
4.5
Place for pocket
2
To be folded
52
1

Pocket　Cut 3
3
12.5
Embroidery area =63 sts
17.5
19.5 = 97 sts
2
21.5
To be folded

To be folded
1
Pocket lining
Cut 3
12
21.5

Wrong side of pocket

Fusible unwoven textile
12.5
19.5

Place the fusible textile on the wrong side of the embroidered piece, and press with iron.

↓

Right side

2
Wrong side

58.5

1 Join with right sides facing, and machine-stitch with 1cm seam allowance.

2 Fold in the edge, and sew up making the lining less obvious from front view.

3 Put edges of front piece on, and sew up in Feather Stitch.

A

Finished Panel

Braided with 3 sets of 24-thread floss, in 37 cm length.

Hanging Cord

Press seam allowances open.

2.5cm

Stitch

1 cm A

Pass the wooden bar through.

B

Sewn to the panel piece with hand.

C

With right sides together, and sew on.

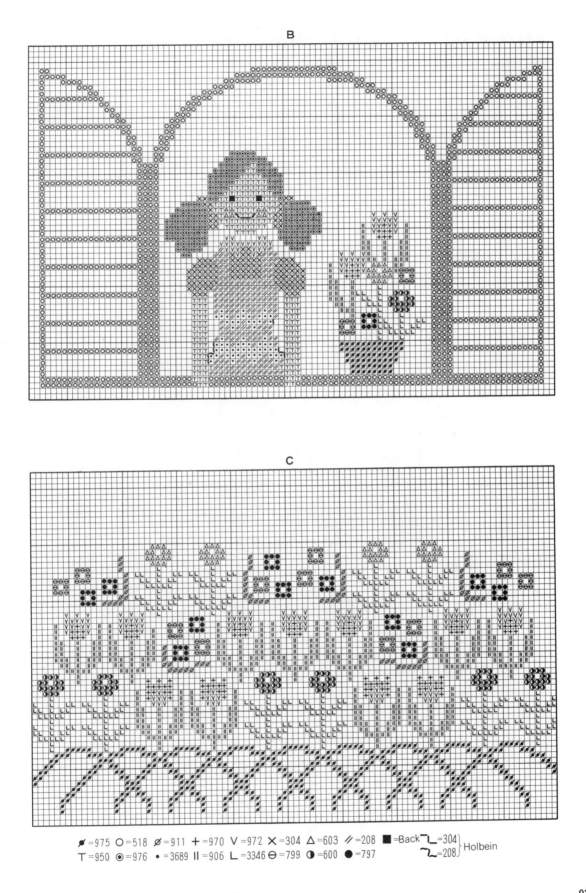

B

C

✎=975 ○=518 ∅=911 +=970 V=972 X=304 △=603 ∥=208 ■=Back ﹂=304 ⎫
T=950 ⊙=976 •=3689 ‖=906 L=3346 ⊖=799 ◑=600 ●=797   ⌐208 ⎬ Holbein
                                                                    ﹋﹋=208 ⎭

FRAMED PICTURE, shown on page 19 (Top)

Materials: Beige Java cloth (60 vertical and horizontal threads per 10 cm square) 31 cm by 27 cm/Ovel-shaped picture frame 21 cm by 17 cm (inside).

THREADS: DMC 6-strand embroidery floss: 1 skein of White; 1/2 skein each of Pistachio Green (368, 367, 320), Ivy Green (500), Moss Green (937), Avocado (470), Laurel Green (988), Scarab Green (3348), Peacock Green (991), Light Warm Tan (738), Red Brown (922), Dark Yellow Gold (725), Cardinal Red (347), Morocco Red (3328), Geranium Red (817, 353, 350), Coral (351), Orange (741), Lemon Yellow (444, 307), Cornflower Blue (794, 793, 792) and Lilac (208); small amount each of Kelly Green (703), Golden Yellow (783), Coffee Brown (801).

Finished size: Same as the frame.

Directions: 1-thread square is counted for each stitch in the chart. Use double strands of floss, and begin working cross-stitches from the center point of the embroidery area. Mount and frame.

S = 988	● = 500	I = 368	C = 3348	P = 367	V = 937	X = 470
O = White	◉ = 783	K = 725	• = 703	■ = 801	✕ = 347	◑ = 817
− = 353	∥ = 320	7 = 307	α = 444	✕ = 741	L = 794	△ = 793

✎ = 991   ◎ = 738   ▲ = 922
◐ = 3328   ℓ = 351   ⟨ = 350
∅ = 208   ✺ = 792

ALBUM, shown on page 20 (Top)

Materials: Light beige Java cloth (36 vertical and horizontal threads per 10 cm square) 90 cm by 40.5 cm.
THREADS: DMC 6-strand embroidery floss: 1 skein each of Beige (3045), Pistachio Green (320), Hot Pink (956), Garnet Red (326, 335), 1/2 skein each of Ivory (704), Soft Pink (818), Ivy Green (501), Scarlet (816), Forget-me-not Blue (826, 813); small amount each of Medium Yellow Orange (743), Hazel-nut Brown (420).
Finished size: 40 cm by 34.5 cm.
Size of stitch: 1 square of design = 1 square mesh of fabric.
Directions: Find the embroidery area, and work with 6 strands of floss. You may need professional help for finished album.

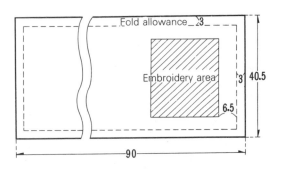

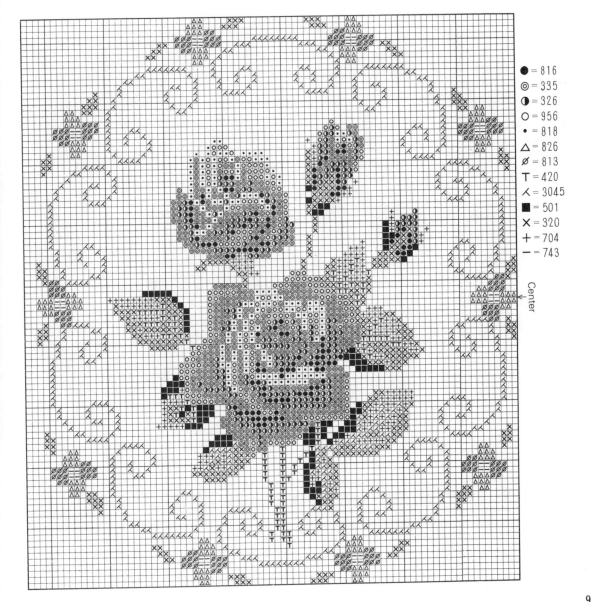

● = 816
◎ = 335
◖ = 326
○ = 956
• = 818
△ = 826
∅ = 813
T = 420
⅄ = 3045
■ = 501
✕ = 320
+ = 704
— = 743

ALBUM, shown on page 20 (Bottom)

Materials: Yellow Aida cloth (35 vertical and horizontal threads per 10 cm square) 86 cm by 35 cm.
THREADS: DMC 6-strand embroidery floss: 2-1/2 skeins of Brilliant Green (702); 2 skeins each of Poppy (666), Cerise (604); 1 skein each of Brilliant Green (700), Royal Blue (995); 1/2 skein each of Tangerine Yellow (740), White; small amount each of Mahogany (300), Umber Gold (976), Plum (550), Brilliant Green (703), Umber (739), Black (310).
Finished size: 38 cm by 29 cm.
Directions: 1-thread square is counted for each stitch in the chart. Find the embroidery area, and work with 6 strands of floss. Professional help may be needed for finished album.

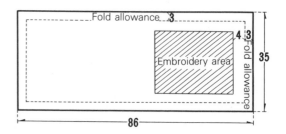

Holbein with 6 strands of floss (995)

Outline with 6 strands of floss (300)

● =700 O =702 V =703 ▲ =550 ◑ =666 △ =740 X =604 T =995 ⊙ =300 ∅ =976 ⋏ =739 ■ =Black •= White

PILLOWS, shown on page 19 (Bottom)

Materials: (for each) Each of Black and Beige Aida cloth (35 vertical and horizontal threads per 10 cm square) 89 cm by 46 cm/Brown silk cord of 1.2 cm-diameter 215 cm/37 cm-long zipper/Fabric for inner pillow 47 cm by 92 cm/Stuffing kapok 460 gr.

THREADS: DMC 6-strand embroidery floss: 2 skeins of Bronze Green (732); 1-1/2 skeins each of Avocado (471), Soft Pink (776), Old Rose (3354); 1 skein each of Copper Green (833, 830), Bronze Green (730), Avocado (469), Garnet Red (309), Magenta Rose (961), Hot Pink

(956), Parakeet Green (906), Scarlet (816), Raspberry Red (3685), Old Rose (3350); 1/2 skein each of Avocado (470), Hot Pink (957), Flesh (951); small amount each of Yellow Green (734), Scarab Green (3348), Parakeet Green (907), Dark Yellow Gold (725).

Finished size: 43 cm square.

Directions: 1-thread square is counted for each stitch in the chart. Use 6 strands of floss, and begin from the center point of the embroidery area. Design of the chart is converted for the second pillow (so that the roses are laid symmetrically). Sew the zipper. Make the pillow, and pass the silk cord around, a loop at each corner.

How to attach the cord

■ = 830
ℓ = 833
△ = 732
▲ = 730
V = 469
+ = 907
P = 906
⟨ = 471
I = 734
X = 470
● = 816
◑ = 309
◎ = 956
• = 776
O = 957
✕ = 3685
∅ = 3350
⊙ = 961
Φ = 3354
□ = 725
7 = 951
S = 3348

Center

Center

PILLOW CASE & BED LINEN, shown on page 21 (Top)

Pillow case

Materials: Checked gingham 88 cm by 73 cm / Green cotton broadcloth 90 cm by 36 cm for frill.
THREADS: DMC 6-strand embroidery floss: 1 skein each of Pistachio Green (890), Dark Yellow Orange (742); 1/2 skein each of Canary Yellow (970), Dark Red Orange (900), Parakeet Green (907, 905).

Finished size: Illustrated.

Directions: Find the embroidery area in the fabric, and work with 3 strands of floss. 1-thread square is counted for each stitch in the chart.

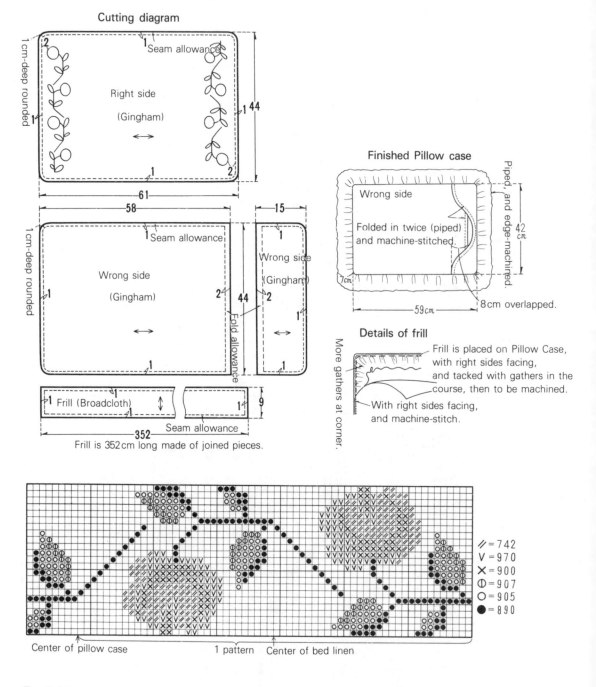

Cutting diagram

1cm-deep rounded

2
1 Seam allowance
Right side
(Gingham)
1 44
61
58
1 Seam allowance
Wrong side
(Gingham)
15
Wrong side
(Gingham)
2 44 2
Fold allowance
Frill (Broadcloth)
9
Seam allowance
352
Frill is 352 cm long made of joined pieces.

Finished Pillow case

Wrong side
Folded in twice (piped) and machine-stitched.
Piped, and edge-machined.
42 cm
7cm
59cm
8cm overlapped.

More gathers at corner.

Details of frill

Frill is placed on Pillow Case, with right sides facing, and tacked with gathers in the course, then to be machined.
With right sides facing, and machine-stitch.

// = 742
V = 970
X = 900
⊕ = 907
O = 905
● = 890

Center of pillow case   1 pattern   Center of bed linen

Bed Linen

Materials: Checked gingham 92 cm by 96 cm / Green cotton broadcloth 92 cm by 17.5 cm for frill.

THREADS: DMC 6-strand embroidery floss: 1/2 skein each of Pistachio Green (890), Canary Yellow (970), Dark

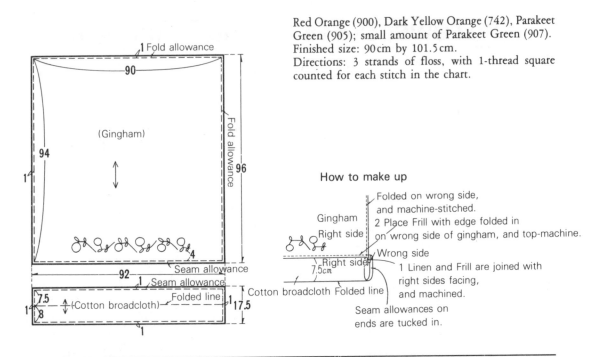

Red Orange (900), Dark Yellow Orange (742), Parakeet Green (905); small amount of Parakeet Green (907).
Finished size: 90 cm by 101.5 cm.
Directions: 3 strands of floss, with 1-thread square counted for each stitch in the chart.

1 Fold allowance
90
(Gingham)
94
Fold allowance
96
1
4
Seam allowance
92
1 Seam allowance
Folded line
7.5
(Cotton broadcloth)
1
8
17.5
1

How to make up

Gingham
Right side
Folded on wrong side, and machine-stitched.
2 Place Frill with edge folded in on wrong side of gingham, and top-machine.
Wrong side
Right side
7.5cm
1 Linen and Frill are joined with right sides facing, and machined.
Cotton broadcloth Folded line
Seam allowances on ends are tucked in.

SLIPPERS, shown on page 21 (Bottom)

Materials: Red Aida cloth (35 vertical and horizontal threads per 10 cm square) 76 cm by 30 cm.
THREADS: DMC 6-strand embroidery floss: 2 skeins of Brilliant Green (700); 1 skein each of Canary Yellow (972), Saffron (726), Brilliant Green (703), White; 1/2 skein each of Flame Red (606), Mahogany (300).
Finished size: Regular size.

Directions: Cut out pieces as illustrated, and work cross-stitches where indicated. Use 6 strands of floss, and count 1-thread square for each stitch in the chart. Professional help may be needed for finished slippers.

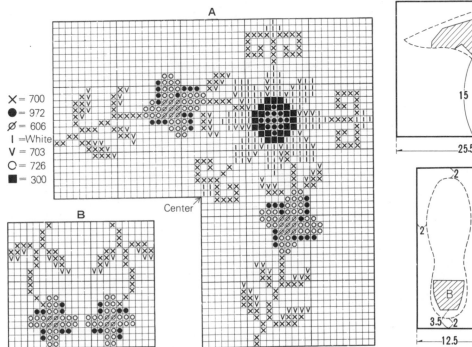

X = 700
● = 972
∅ = 606
I = White
V = 703
O = 726
■ = 300

A

B

Center

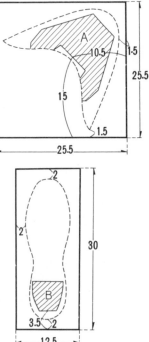

A
10.5
1.5
25.5
15
1.5
25.5

2
2
2
30
B
3.5 2
12.5

PILLOWS, shown on page 23 (Bottom)

Materials for one: Red Java cloth (36 vertical and horizontal threads per 10 cm square) 83 cm 43 cm/ Fabric for inner pillow 86 cm by 44 cm/37 cm-long zipper/340 gr kapok.

THREADS: DMC 6-strand embroidery floss:

Left Pillow

5-1/2 skeins of White; 3-1/2 skeins of Lemon Yellow (307); 1 skein each of Orange (741), Fuschia Pink (603),

Cerise (605); small amount each of Dark Blue (797), Emerald Green (911), Fire Red (946), Episcopal Purple (917).

Right Pillow

5-1/2 skeins of White; 3-1/2 skeins of Electric Blue (996); 1 skein each of Kelly Green (700), Parakeet Green (907), Royal Blue (820), Fuschia Pink (603), small amount each of Royal Blue (797), Emerald Green (911), Fire Red

Left pillow

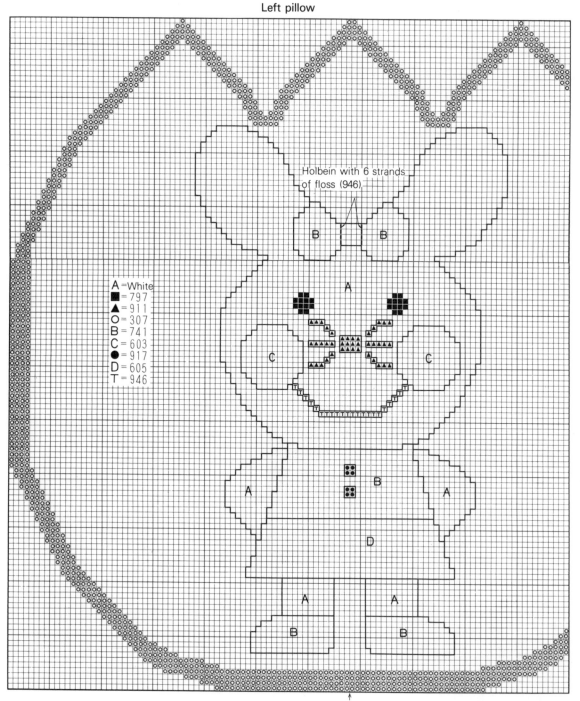

Holbein with 6 strands of floss (946)

A = White
■ = 797
▲ = 911
O = 307
B = 741
C = 603
● = 917
D = 605
T = 946

Center

(946), Episcopal Purple (917).
Finished size: 40 cm square.
Size of stitch: 1 square of design = 1 square mesh of fabric.
Directions: Find the embroidery area, and work with 6 strands of floss throughout. To make up Pillow, sew in the zipper first, and put inner pillow in. (Corners of the inner pillow are slightly rounded.)

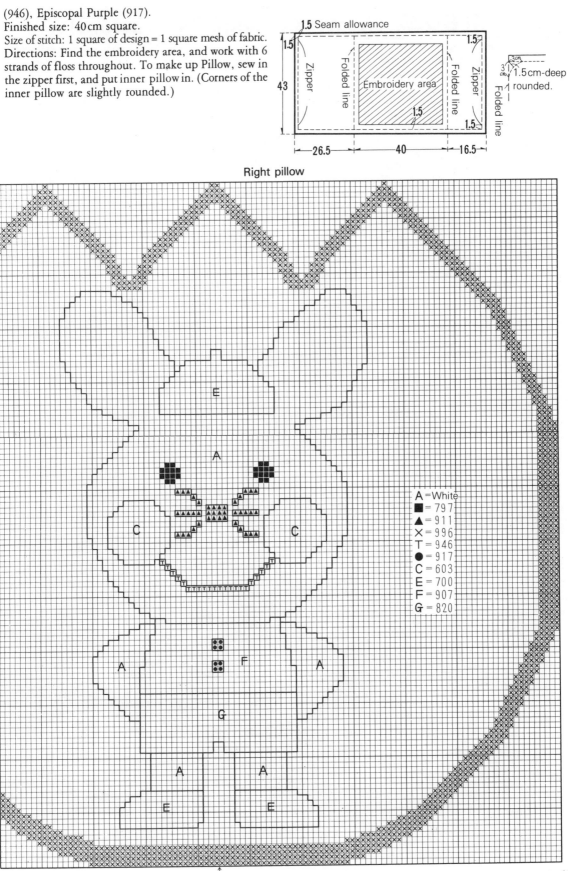

Right pillow

A =White
■ = 797
▲ = 911
X = 996
T = 946
● = 917
C = 603
E = 700
F = 907
G = 820

Center

ALBUM, shown on page 24 (Bottom)

Materials: Blue Indian cloth (51 vertical and horizontal threads per 10 cm) 86 cm by 35 cm.
THREADS: DMC 6-strand embroidery floss: 4 skeins of Cerise (604); 1-1/2 skeins of Episcopal Purple (718); 1 skein each of Raspberry Red (3688), Sévres Blue (798), White, Lemon Yellow (445), Soft Pink (819), Brilliant Green (704); 1/2 skein each of Cornflower Blue (791),

Cerise (600), Episcopal Purple (917), Raspberry Red (3689), Geranium Red (892), Plum (552), Emerald Green (955), Fire Red (946), Tangerine Yellow (740); small amount each of Royal Blue (996, 995), Flame Red (606), Brilliant Green (703, 701) and Peacock Green (992).
Finished size: 38 cm by 29 cm.

Holbein with
4 strands (798)

(606) 2 strands
(3688) 2 strands

Center

Holbein with
3 strands (704)

Holbein with
3 strands (992)

■ =791	◐ =3689
+ =995	⊗ =892
◖ =996	■ =606
∧ =798	I =819
— =White	△ =552
L =445	T =701
● =600	V =703
○ =604	╳ =704
◎ =917	◇ =955
╱ =718	▲ =946
Ø =3688	╳ =740

Directions: 1-thread square is counted for each stitch in the chart. Use 4 strands of floss throughout. Better ask professional help for finishing the album.

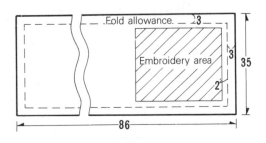

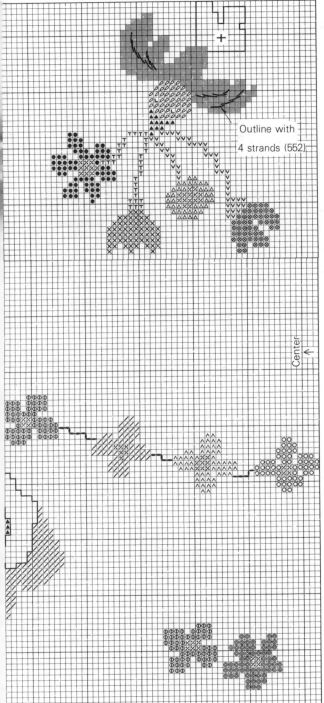

Outline with
4 strands (552)

Center

ALBUM, shown on page 24 (Top)

Materials: Beige Aida cloth (35 vertical and horizontal threads per 10 cm square) 90 cm by 40.5 cm.
THREADS: DMC 6-strand embroidery floss: 1 skein each of Geranium Red (754), Parma Violet (209), Garnet Red (335); 1/2 skein each of Emerald Green (910), Kelly Green (702), Parakeet Green (906), Dark Yellow Orange (742), Medium Yellow Orange (743), Umber Gold (976), Cranberry Red (321), Forget-me-not Blue (826, 813); small amount each of Cinnamon Orange (975), Black (310), Garnet Red (309).
Finished size: 40 cm by 34.5 cm.
Size of stitch: 1 square of design = 1 square mesh of fabric.
Directions: Find the embroidery area in the fabric, and work with 6 strands of floss. Professional help may be needed for finishing the album.

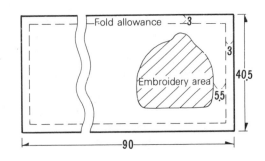

(Continued next.)

Holbein (976)

※ = 910
X = 702
% = 906
🍃 = 742
L = 743
▲ = 975
△ = 976
■ = Black
● = 321
◎ = 309
O = 335
— = 209
• = 754
+ = 826
I = 813

Holbein (Black)

Center

PILLOW, shown on page 18

Materials: Each of Beige and Black Java cloth (36 vertical and horizontal threads per 10 cm square) 90 cm by 46.5 cm/Fabric for each inner pillow 46.5 cm by 92 cm/2 36 cm-long zipper/450 gr kapok for each pillow.
THREADS: DMC 6-strand embroidery floss: 5 skeins of Geranium Red (892); 2 skeins each of Turkey Red (321), Flame Red (606), Canary Yellow (971); 1-1/2 skeins each of Brilliant Green (703), Peacock Green (992); 1 skein each of Poppy (666), Cerise (602, 601), Plum (552), Fire Red (947); 1/2 skein each of Brilliant Green (704), Tangerine Yellow (742), Indigo (336), Royal Blue (996, 995), Parma Violet (208); small amount each of Royal Blue (797), Peacock Green (993), Cerise (604). DMC embroidery floss, No. 5: 6 skeins of Red.
Finished size: 43 cm by 42.5 cm.
Directions: 1-thread square is counted for each stitch in the chart. Find the center point of the embroidery area, and begin working cross-stitch with 6 strands of floss. To finish the pillows, first sew in zipper, then put the inner

pillow inside. The corners of the pillows are slightly notched in the course of machine-stitching. (See illustration.) Make tassels with #5 embroidery floss.

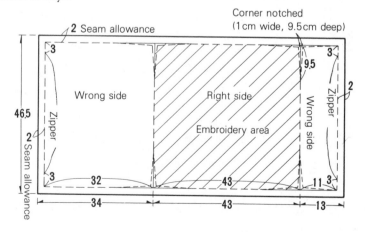

104

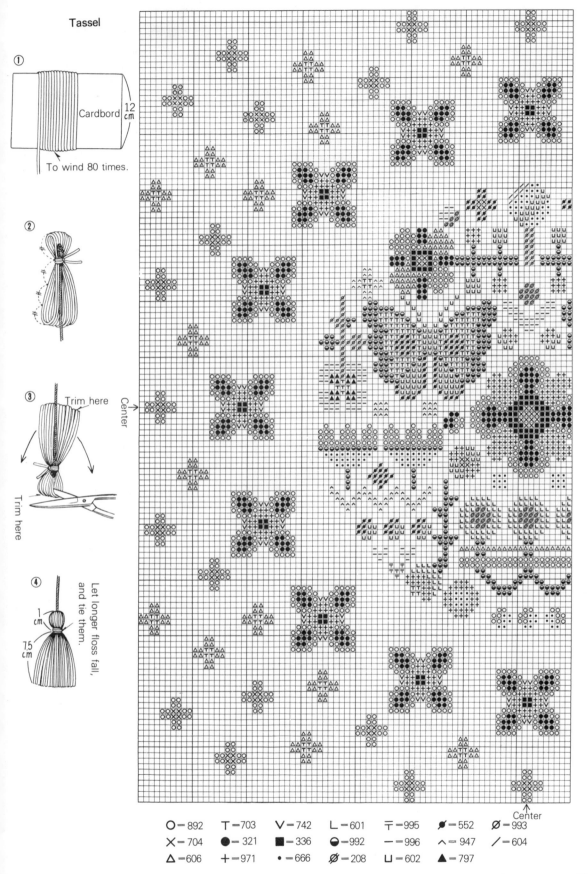

Tassel

① Cardbord 12 cm

To wind 80 times.

②

③ Trim here

Center

Trim here

④ 1 cm

7.5 cm

Let longer floss fall, and tie them.

O = 892　T = 703　V = 742　L = 601　⊤ = 995　✦ = 552　Ø = 993

X = 704　● = 321　■ = 336　◒ = 992　— = 996　^ = 947　╱ = 604

△ = 606　+ = 971　• = 666　∅ = 208　⊔ = 602　▲ = 797

Center

WALL HANGING, shown on page 7 (Top)

Materials: Beige Java cloth (36 vertical and horizontal threads per 10 cm square) 51.5 cm by 42 cm/ # 25 Embroidery floss; 5 skeins of Wine Rose and 2 skeins of Beige/ # 8 Embroidery floss in Beige for fringes 30 gr./Beige fabric for lining 46 cm by 30 cm/ # F Crochet hook/Bar with 1 cm-diameter hole through 34 cm.
THREADS: DMC 6-strand embroidery floss: 5 skeins of Raspberry Red (3687); 2 skeins of Dark Brown (3033). DMC cotton thread No. 20: 30 gr of Beige.
Finished size: 47 cm by 34 cm, excluding the tasseles.

Directions: 1-thread square is counted for each stitch in the chart. Find the center point of the embroidery area, and work with 4 strands of floss. Join the embroidered piece with lining, with the right sides facing, and machine-stitch the vertical sides. Fold in 2.5 cm of the top edge. Finish the bottom edge also with hand, making the lining less obvious front view.

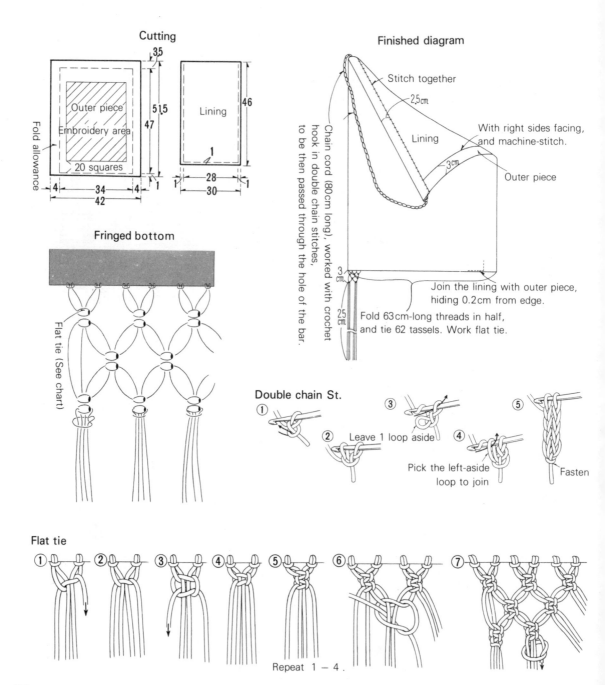

Cutting

35

Outer piece

Embroidery area

20 squares

Fold allowance

51.5

47

4 — 34 — 4

42

1

Lining

46

28

30

1

1

Finished diagram

Stitch together

2.5 cm

Lining

With right sides facing, and machine-stitch.

Outer piece

3 cm

Chain cord (80 cm long), worked with crochet hook in double chain stitches, to be then passed through the hole of the bar.

3 cm

Join the lining with outer piece, hiding 0.2 cm from edge.

25 cm

Fold 63 cm-long threads in half, and tie 62 tassels. Work flat tie.

Fringed bottom

Flat tie (See chart)

Double chain St.

① ② Leave 1 loop aside ③ ④ Pick the left-aside loop to join ⑤ Fasten

Flat tie

① ② ③ ④ ⑤ ⑥ ⑦

Repeat 1 — 4.

106

Center

Center

X=3687

WALL POCKETS, shown on page 23 (Top)

Materials: Black Java cloth (28 vertical and horizontal threads per 10 cm square) 34 cm by 25 cm / Green denim panel 70 cm by 41 cm / White cotton fabric for lining 70 cm by 41 cm / 2 45 cm long bars with 1 cm-diameter hole through / 40 eyelets (available at speciality shop) / 70 cm long linen cord.

THREADS: DMC 6-strand embroidery floss: 1 skein of Parakeet Green (905); 1/2 skein each of Lemon Yellow (445, 444), Electric Blue (996, 995), Dark Lilac (550), Plum (553), Geranium Red (350), Cranberry Red (321), Parakeet Green (907); small amount each of Kelly Green (700), Geranium Red (353).

Finished size: 38cm by 33cm.

Size of stitch: 1 square of design = 1 square mesh of fabric.

Directions: Cut java cloth pieces as indicated, and find the embroidery area in each piece. Work with 6 strands of floss throughout. Place embroidered pieces on the denim panel, and sew on with machine-stitches. Leave top edges of A and B, making pockets. Join the pocketed piece with lining, with right sides facing, machine-stitch both vertical sides. Put in the eyelets. Pass the holed bar through the top and bottom, as illustrated. To finish, cast the linen cord on the top bar. You may need professional help for putting the eyelets in.

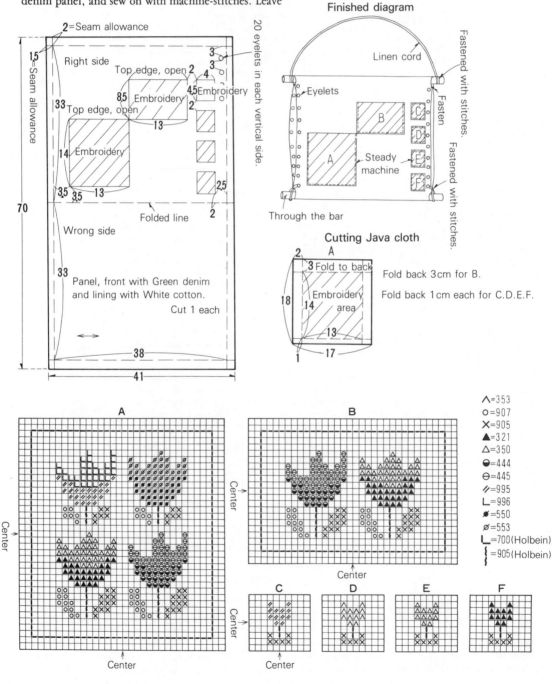

108

ALBUM, shown on page 37 (Top)

Materials: Navy blue Java cloth (36 vertical and horizontal threads per 10 cm square) 86 cm by 35 cm.
THREADS: DMC 6-strand embroidery floss: 1 skein each of Cerise (603), Garnet red (326), Raspberry Red (3689), Peacock Green (991), Yellow Green (732), Scarab Green (3348); 1/2 skein each of Plum (552), Canary Yellow (972), Royal Blue (996), Red Brown (919).
Finished size: 38 cm by 29 cm.
Directions: 1-thread square is counted for each stitch in the chart. Find the embroidery area in the fabric, and work with 6 strands of floss throughout. You may need professional help for finishing the album.

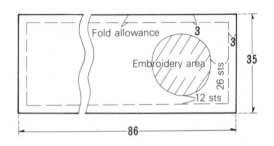

● = 326
○ = 603
• = 3689
人 = 996
∧ = 552
✔ = 972
× = 991
╱ = 732
— = 3348
■ = 919

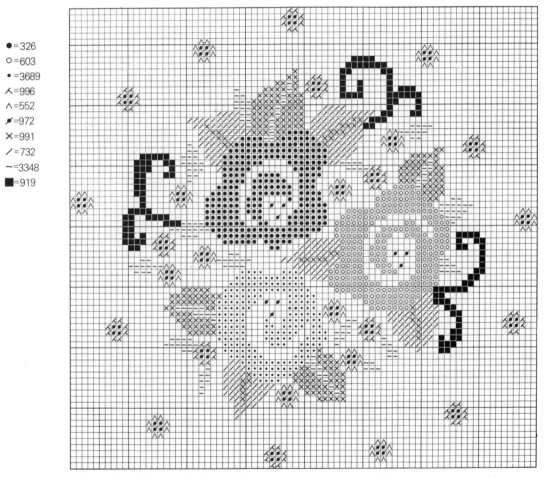

ALBUM, shown on page 37 (Bottom)

Materials: Green Aida cloth (35 vertical and horizontal threads per 10 cm square) 86 cm by 35 cm.
THREADS: DMC 6-strand embroidery floss: 4 skeins each of Flame Red (606), White; 1-1/2 skeins of Mahogany (300); 1 skein each of Canary Yellow (972), Umber Gold (976); 1/2 skein each of Peacock Green (991), Brilliant Green (703), Moss Green (472); small amount each of Fire Red (946), Royal Blue (995), Umber (739), Black (310).
Finished size: 38 cm by 29 cm.
Directions: 1-thread square is counted for each stitch in the chart. Work with 6 strands of floss throughout. Professional help may be needed for finished album.

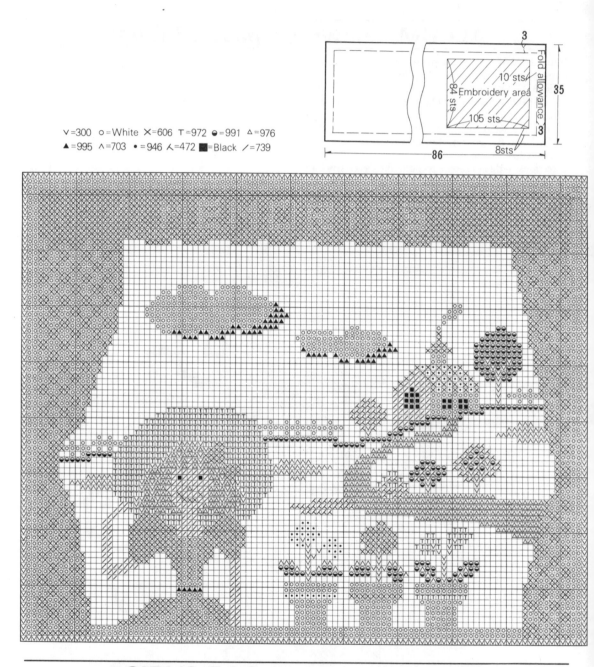

V=300 o=White ✕=606 ⊤=972 ●=991 △=976
▲=995 ∧=703 •=946 ⅄=472 ■=Black ╱=739

GIRL'S BAG, shown on page 45

Materials: Red Java cloth (36 vertical and horizontal threads per 10 cm square) 81 cm by 39.5 cm/Red cotton fabric for lining 63 cm by 37.5 cm.
THREADS: DMC 6-strand embroidery floss: 2 skeins each of White, Sky Blue (518); 1-1/2 skeins each of Scarab Green (3347), Drab (613); 1 skein each of Sky Blue (517), Umber (433), Brilliant Green (699), Royal Blue (796), Golden Yellow (782), Saffron (725); 1/2 skein each of Drab (612), Soft Pink (818).
Finished size: 34.5 cm widthwise, 29.5 cm down.
Directions: 1-thread square is counted for each stitch in the chart. Use 6 strands of floss throughout. Make Bag with embroidered piece. Make an inner bag same way, and join with front bag with machine, with two straps inserted in the course.

Cutting

Strap (2 pieces)

Machine-stitch

3.5cm finished width

1 — 1

39.5

Seam allowance

9

Fold allowance

2

Embroidery area

29.5

14 sts

Bottom

1.5

1.5

29.5

Seam allowance

2

Fold allowance

37.5

63

Handle

Slightly in to make less obvious from front.

0.7cm   4cm

8cm

Straps are inserted the between front and lining of the bag.

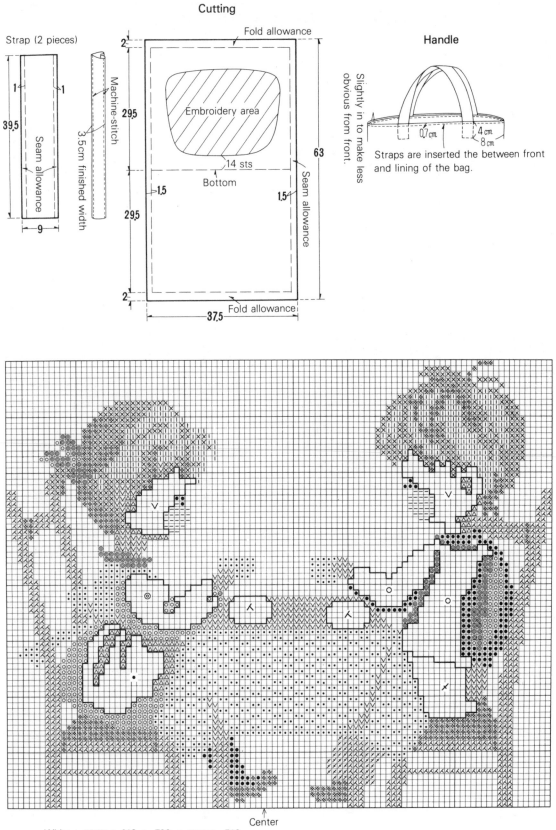

Center

•=White 人=3347 V=613 ●=796 ◎=517 ○=518

✳=433 ✗=699 △=612 −=818 X=782 I=725

PILLOWS, shown on page 29

Materials for one: Beige Java cloth (36 vertical and horizontal threads per 10cm square) 44cm square/ Heavyweight cotton fabric for lining 47cm by 44cm/ Fabric for inner pillow 88cm by 45cm/41cm-long zipper/420gr kapok.

THREADS: DMC 6-strand embroidery floss:

Left Pillow

2-1/2 skeins each of Drab (613), Geranium Pink (891); 1-1/2 skeins of Geranium Pink (893); 1 skein each of Geranium Pink (892), Hot Pink (957, 956), Magenta Rose (963), Scarlet (304), Garnet Red (309), Dark Yellow Gold (725), Canary Yellow (972), Lemon Yellow (307); 1/2 skein each of Raspberry Red (3688, 3687), Old Rose (3354), Forget-me-not Blue (813), Electric Blue (996), Parma Violet (211, 209), Ivory (704).

Right Pillow

2-1/2 skeins each of Drab (613), Electric Blue (995); 1-1/2 skeins of Electric Blue (996); 1 skein each of Royal Blue (796), Sévres Blue (798), Forget-me-not Blue (826, 813), Peacock Blue (517), Baby Blue (800), Dark Yellow Gold (725), Canary Yellow (972), Lemon Yellow (307); 1/2 skein each of Antique Blue (930, 932), Cornflower Blue (794), Parma Violet (211, 209), Ivory (704), Hot Pink (957), Geranium Pink (891).

Finished size: 41cm square.

Size of stitch: 1 square of design = 1 square mesh of fabric.

Directions: Find the center point of the embroidery area in the fabric, and work with 6 strands of floss. To finish, sew in zipper before machining the sides of the pillow. Inner pillow is stuffed with kapok.

	Left	Right
■ =	304	796
• =	892	798
⊗ =	956	826
◑ =	957	813
● =	309	517
◥ =	891	995
◎ =	893	996
◍ =	963	800
▲ =	3687	930
△ =	3688	932
◇ =	3354	794
+ =	725	
V =	972	
∧ =	307	
T =	211	Common to all
⊙ =	209	
L =	704	
✕ =	613	
◎ =	813	957
⬚ =	996	891

Center →

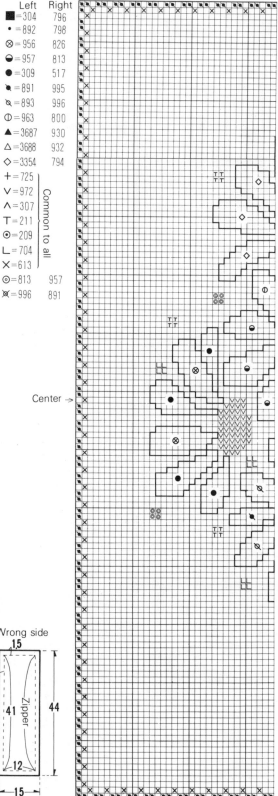

Cutting

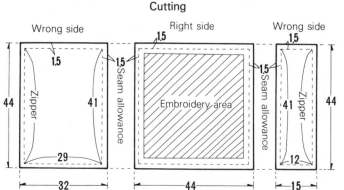

Wrong side

1.5

1.5

Zipper

44

41

29

Right side

1.5

1.5 Seam allowance

Embroidery area

Wrong side

1.5

1.5 Seam allowance

Zipper

41

44

12

32

44

15

Center

ALBUM, shown on page 36 (Top)

Materials: Beige Indian cloth (51 vertical and horizontal threads per 10 cm square) 90 cm by 40.5 cm.

THREADS: DMC 6-strand embroidery floss: 1 skein each of Fushchia Pink (604), Cerise (605), Kelly Green (703), Ivory (704), Watermelon Pink (894); 1/2 skein each of Scarab Green (3348, 3347, 3346), Avocado (469), Parakeet Green (907, 906), Golden Yellow (783, 782), Dark Yellow Gold (725), Canary Yellow (973, 972), Hot Pink (956), Forget-me-not Blue (827), Coffee Brown (801), Fuschia Pink (601), Geranium Pink (891), Saffron (727), Pistachio Green (368), Lemon Yellow (445), Tangerine Yellow (740) and Ivy Green (500).

Finished size: 40 cm by 34.5 cm.

Directions: 1-thread square is counted for each stitch in the chart. Use 3 strands of floss. Find the center point of the embroidery area, and begin working center roses first. Professinal help may be needed for finished album.

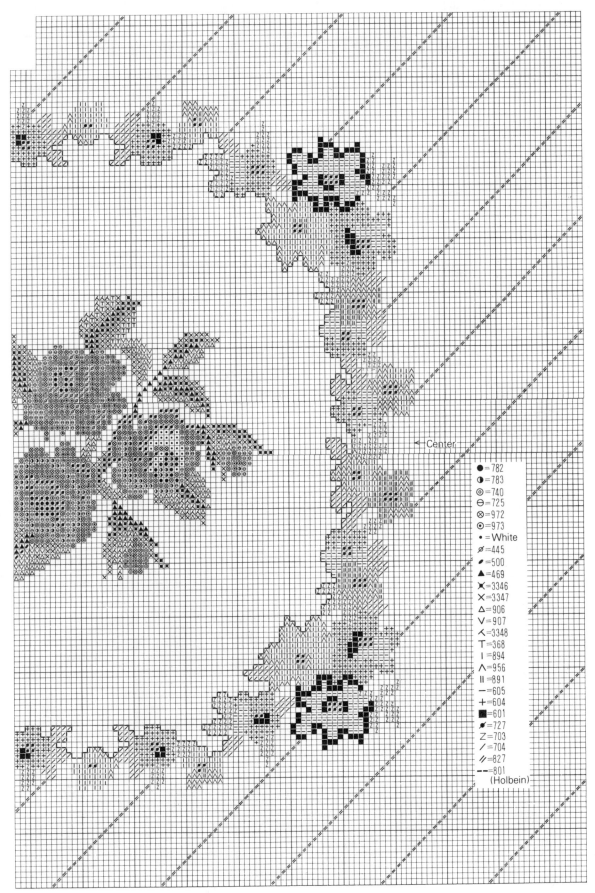

← Center

● = 782
◐ = 783
◉ = 740
⊖ = 725
⊗ = 972
⊙ = 973
• = White
∅ = 445
◢ = 500
▲ = 469
✱ = 3346
✕ = 3347
△ = 906
∨ = 907
✕ = 3348
T = 368
I = 894
∧ = 956
‖ = 891
— = 605
+ = 604
■ = 601
✔ = 727
Z = 703
⁄ = 704
∥ = 827
−− = 801
(Holbein)

115

TABLECLOTH, shown on page 12

Materials: White Ajour cloth 107.5 cm by 52.5 cm.
THREADS: DMC 6-strand embroidery floss: 5 skeins of
Corn Yellow (712); 1 skein each of Soft Pink (899, 776),
Pistachio Green (368, 367, 320), Medium Yellow Orange
(743), Light Yellow Orange (744); 1/2 skein each of
Garnet Red (335, 326, 309), Geranium Pink (892), Dark
Yellow Orange (742), Dark Yellow Gold (725); small
amount of Tangerine Yellow (740).
Finished size: 98.5 cm by 43.5 cm.
Directions: 2-thread square is counted for each stitch in
the chart. Find the embroidery area in the fabric, and
work four-side stitches for diagonal squares with double
strands of floss, and cross-stitches for roses with 3 strands
of floss. The direction of the roses are changed as illustrated. Garnish the squares with satin stitches with
4 strands of floss. To outline the embroidered area, work
hem stitches, with the corners mitered.

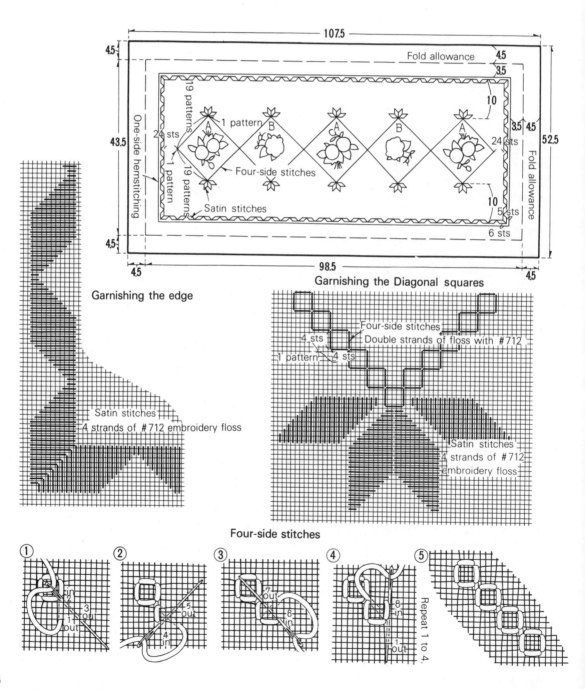

Garnishing the edge

Garnishing the Diagonal squares

Four-side stitches

Repeat 1 to 4.

116

A

B

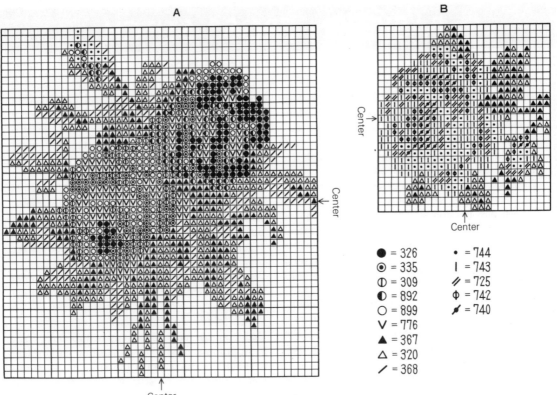

Center

Center

Center

Center

● = 326   • = 744
⊙ = 335   I = 743
⧇ = 309   ⫽ = 725
◑ = 892   Φ = 742
○ = 899   ✦ = 740
V = 776
▲ = 367
△ = 320
╱ = 368

BASICS IN CROSS-STITCH

FABRICS

The exact amount of the fabric to make each project is given in this book. Make sure to buy enough fabric, allowing for shrinkage or difference of thread count.

Fineness or coarseness of the fabric will determine the finished size of the design.

To make the project the size shown in the book, use fabric with same gauge (the number of vertical and horizontal threads per 10cm square is given in the book). If you use coarser fabric than indicated, the finished size will be bigger and you may need more fabric. There are several kinds of fabric suitable for cross-stitch embroidery.

Cotton and linen fabrics on which you can count the threads easily are used most. Woolen and polyester fabrics are also used. Choose the most suitable even-weave fabric for your project.

Indian cloth and Java canvas are woven with several threads to each warp and weft. They are the most suitable fabrics for cross-stitch embroidery.

Congress canvas in woven with a single thick thread, thus this is a heavy-weight canvas. It is often used for cross-stitch embroidery and free-style embroidery with large stitches. Lightweight congress canvas is used for table-cloths with complicated embroidery.

Oxford cloth is often used for counted thread embroidery. This is an even-weave fabric and has double threads.

Even-weave linen comes in various thickness from fine to coarse. Lightweight linen is used for table linens with fine embroidery.

Length of Thread:

Use thread of 50cm length at a time, since longer thread may become tangled or twisted, which causes poor results and also causes the thread to lose its shine.

Starting Point:

Count the threads of the fabric and mark the starting point or center of design with colored thread. Make sure to count the threads of the fabric when embroidering repeating or symmetrical patterns.

THREADS

There are various kinds of threads used, depending on the thickness of the fabric.

Six-strand embroidery floss, No. 25, is most commonly used. Woolen yarn (tapestry yarn), and gold and silver threads are also used according to the texture of the fabric.

Six-strand embroidery floss, No. 25: This can be separated into one or more strands. When 3 strands of floss are required, for example, pull out one strand at a time and put three strands together. The length of one skein is 8 meters long.

Pearl cotton, No. 5: This is a shiny corded thread. The length of one skein is 25 meters long.

NEEDLES

You may use any needle for embroidery, but a blunt-pointed needle for cross-stitch embroidery is easiest to use. Change the size of the needle and the number of strands, depending on the fabric to be used.

To embroider with one strand of floss, use No. 23 needle for cross-stitch embroidery, and Nos. 19 and 20 needles for 4 to 6 strands of floss. Choose the proper needle and the number of strands suitable for the fabric and design.

Preparations:

The fabric suitable for cross-stitch embroidery frays easily, so overcast the edges with large stitches to prevent raveling.

How to Thread:

Fold the thread over the end of the needle, slip it off with thumb and forefinger and push it through the needle eye.

Fold the thread end.   Slip it off with thumb and forefinger.

To prevent the thread from twisting:

The thread is apt to twist while embroidering. To prevent this, turn the needle occasionally. Before starting, put the required number of strands together by pulling out one strand at a time from skein.

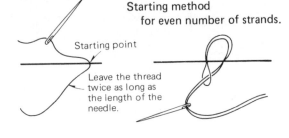

Turn the needle to prevent the thread from twisting.

Starting and Ending:

Leave the thread twice as long as the length of the needle on the wrong side when starting. After embroidering, weave the thread end into 2- to 3cm-stitches on the wrong side and clip off the excess thread. When you use various kinds of colored threads, weave and clip off any excess thread every time new thread is used.

Starting method
for even number of strands.

Starting point

Leave the thread twice as long as the length of the needle.

CROSS-STITCH

Make sure to work all the top threads of crosses in the same direction.
Never mix them up.

To work horizontally:

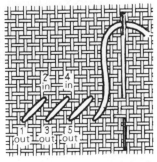

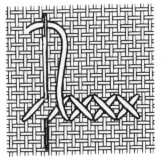

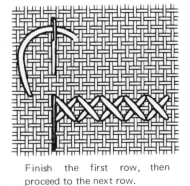

Bring the thread through on the lower left line of the cross. Insert the needle on the upper line a little to the right.

When coming to the end of the row, bring the thread through on the lower right line of the cross and insert the needle on the upper line a little to the left. Return in this way completing the other half of the cross.

Finish the first row, then proceed to the next row.

To complete each cross horizontally:

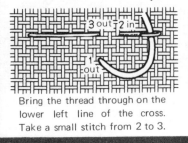

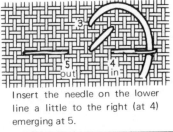

Bring the thread through on the lower left line of the cross. Take a small stitch from 2 to 3.

Insert the needle on the lower line a little to the right (at 4) emerging at 5.

Continue working horizontally completing each cross.

To complete each cross vertically:

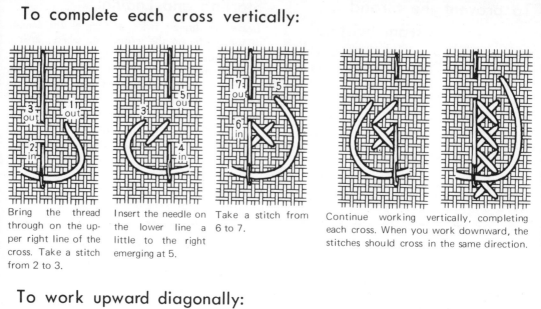

Bring the thread through on the upper right line of the cross. Take a stitch from 2 to 3.

Insert the needle on the lower line a little to the right emerging at 5.

Take a stitch from 6 to 7.

Continue working vertically, completing each cross. When you work downward, the stitches should cross in the same direction.

To work upward diagonally:

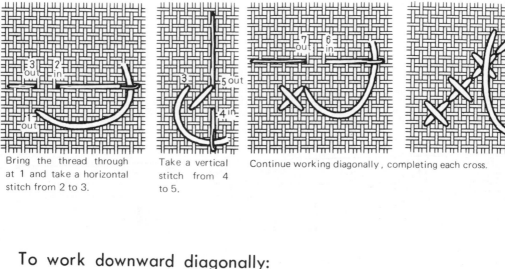

Bring the thread through at 1 and take a horizontal stitch from 2 to 3.

Take a vertical stitch from 4 to 5.

Continue working diagonally, completing each cross.

To work downward diagonally:

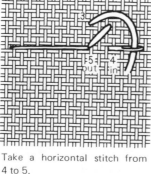

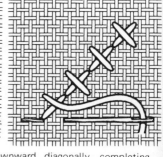

Bring the thread through at 1 and take a vertical stitch from 2 to 3.

Take a horizontal stitch from 4 to 5.

Continue working downward diagonally, completing each cross.

DOUBLE CROSS-STITCH

Work Cross-Stitch first. Then work another Cross-Stitch over the previous stitch as shown. All stitches should cross in the same way.

HOLBEIN STITCH

This is also called Line Stitch and is sometimes used as an outline to Cross-Stitch. The stitch is completed by working from left to right and coming back from right to left. Stitches on the wrong side are the same on the front.

Straight Line:

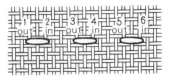

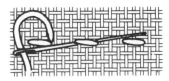

Work running stitch of equal length.

When you come to the end of the row, return in the same way filling in the spaces left by the first row. For a neater finish, work in the same way when you insert the needle and bring it through.

Diagonal Line:

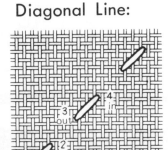

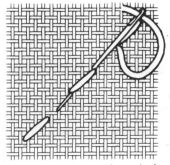

Work running stitch of equal length diagonally.

When you come to the end of the row, return in the same way filling in the spaces left by the first row.

Zigzag Line:

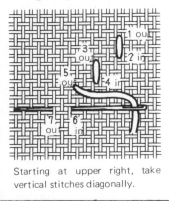

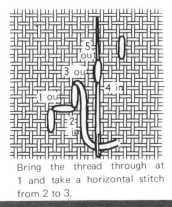

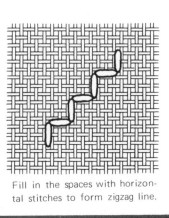

Starting at upper right, take vertical stitches diagonally.

Bring the thread through at 1 and take a horizontal stitch from 2 to 3.

Fill in the spaces with horizontal stitches to form zigzag line.

HOW TO MAKE HEM

Hem-stitch

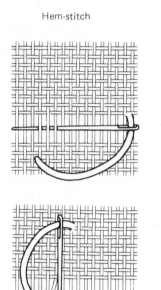

1. Draw out required number of threads from the fabric in both directions.
2. Miter corners and slip-stitch. Baste four sides.
3. Hem-stitch along drawn thread line. (Buttonhole-stitch at corners.)

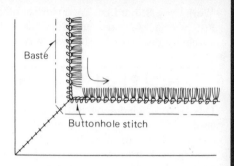

Baste

Buttonhole stitch

Bring the needle out close to the drawn thread line and pick up threads from right to left. Bring the needle in vertically and pull the thread in needle taut. Repeat these steps.

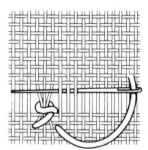

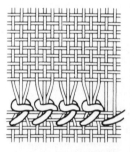

MITERED CORNER

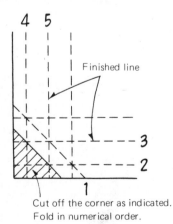

Finished line

4 5

3

2

1

Cut off the corner as indicated.
Fold in numerical order.

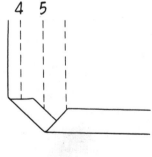

4 5

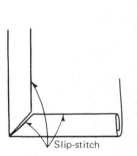

Slip-stitch